More Praise for *It Takes More than Casual Fridays and Free Coffee*

"Diane Adams is a magician when it comes to transforming culture in companies. She recognizes that to preserve the value in mergers—large and small—the billions or millions spent will only lead to a successful outcome if the cultures of the entire enterprise are aligned. Values matter as *It Takes More than Casual Fridays and Free Coffee* clearly illustrates."

—*Lee Shapiro, Managing Partner of 7wire Ventures*

"Diane knows well that our people make the difference. That's why creating a culture that values its team members and their contributions is so important to personal and company success. With *It Takes More than Casual Fridays and Free Coffee*, Diane clearly and simply spells out how you, too, can create that kind of a positive values-based culture in your organization."

—*Michael A. Nemeroff, President and CEO of Chicago-based Vedder Price, a global legal firm*

"In today's business environment, emphasis on culture is the most important part of creating a successful and sustainable business. Diane Adams is one of those rare individuals who truly connects with that. More than ever before, employees care about being a part of something much more meaningful than only their compensation. They want to connect with a set of values and ideals that make them better people. Culture creates that platform to evolve and grow every aspect of a business."

—*Sepideh Saidi, Founder and President of SEPI Engineering Group, one of the most successful engineering firms in North Carolina*

"The world is changing so rapidly, so quickly, and in so many ways. Priority number 1 for any company has to be to have the right culture in place to take on the challenges today. The right culture is one that says, 'We're in this together.' This is Diane's specialty—building cultures and companies where everyone is motivated and driving towards a common goal."

—*Brad Wilson, CEO of Blue Cross Blue Shield of North Carolina*

"Diane Adams is THE expert when it comes to getting culture right in your company."

—*Stedman Graham, entrepreneur, speaker, and* New York Times *and* Wall Street Journal *best-selling author*

It Takes More than Casual Fridays and Free Coffee

Building a Business Culture That Works for Everyone

Diane K. Adams

IT TAKES MORE THAN CASUAL FRIDAYS AND FREE COFFEE

First published in 2015 by
PALGRAVE MACMILLAN®
in the United States—a division of St. Martin's Press LLC,
175 Fifth Avenue, New York, NY 10010.

Where this book is distributed in the UK, Europe and the rest of the world,
this is by Palgrave Macmillan, a division of Macmillan Publishers Limited,
registered in England, company number 785998, of Houndmills,
Basingstoke, Hampshire RG21 6XS.

Palgrave Macmillan is the global academic imprint of the above companies
and has companies and representatives throughout the world.

Palgrave® and Macmillan® are registered trademarks in the United States,
the United Kingdom, Europe and other countries.

ISBN: 978–1–137–52694–6

Library of Congress Cataloging-in-Publication Data

Adams, Diane K.
    It takes more than casual Fridays and free coffee : building a business
culture that works for everyone / by Diane K. Adams.
        pages cm
    Includes bibliographical references and index.
    ISBN 978–1–137–52694–6 (hardcover : alk. paper)
        1. Corporate culture. 2. Organizational behavior. I. Title.

HD58.7.A3135 2015
658.3'12—dc23   2015001267

A catalogue record of the book is available from the British Library.

Design by Newgen Knowledge Works (P) Ltd., Chennai, India.

First edition: August 2015

10 9 8 7 6 5 4 3 2 1

Printed in the United States of America.

This book is dedicated to my amazing parents, Lewis and Barbara Kearney, who showed me the value of "staying true to your values"; to my children, Kristen, Jordan and Danielle, each unique and beautiful, who remind me every day the importance of loving and embracing them for who they are; and to my family and friends who believed in me more than I believed in myself.

Everyone is created with the potential to be extraordinary. Working in a company with a strong values-based culture that believes in individual potential can create an environment to do just that.

—Diane K. Adams

Contents

Part III Being Intentional

About the Author

Author Diane K. Adams knows what it takes to help people and companies grow positive cultures and in turn sustain growth. One of the top names in her field, she has spent more than 25 years at the helm of Human Resources organizations at Fortune 500 companies. Chief executives of smaller companies, and international and national organizations and leaders also regularly tap her expertise as coach, consultant, and/or lecturer to help them hone their positive cultures.

Adams has built values-based, high-performance cultures that endure at companies including Cisco Systems (Nasdaq: CSCO) and Allscripts Healthcare Solutions (Nasdaq: MDRX).

More than a "Human Resources" executive, Adams is a "Culture and Talent" expert. She specializes in helping companies recognize what's required to energize their people and to achieve long-term success at the bottom line.

At Cisco, for example, she joined the company when it had just 4,500 employees. Her roles—including Vice President Human Resources/International, and Vice President Human Resources/Worldwide Sales—revolved around helping ensure that the company could scale successfully. By the time she left 14 years later, Cisco had successfully grown to 70,000 employees in 152 countries.

At Allscripts as Executive Vice President of Culture and Talent, Adams was instrumental in enabling that company to scale its operations from $500 million to $1.44 billion.

Currently, Adams is Chief People Officer at Qlik (Nasdaq: QLIK), one of the fastest-growing high-tech companies worldwide, with nearly 2,200 employees in 30 countries. Her charge is to help accelerate the company's growth beyond $1 billion in revenues (that's almost double current revenues), while still maintaining a global culture with people who care about making a difference with customers and in the community.

Additionally, Adams's role includes making sure Qlik also provides commensurate giveback. In other words, she's charged with ensuring that Qlik's products and services touch the lives of more than 1 billion people. Last year Qlik gave away millions of dollars of its business analytics software to charities and educational institutions worldwide.

Adams also has helmed a successful consultancy focused on organizational and leadership development and excellence.

Adams strives to live her values in her personal life. Reflecting her belief in social responsibility, she's an active and honored member of the International Board of Directors for the Juvenile Diabetes Research Foundation. She's also a member of other boards, including the Make-a-Wish Foundation, Center for Entrepreneurial Development, Communities in Schools of North Carolina, and previously served on the University of North Carolina (UNC) Board of Visitors.

Adams is a graduate in Business Administration from the University of North Carolina.

Introduction

Culture is *the* game changer. Get the culture right, and a company and its people thrive. Miss the mark, and you lose.

Culture is the set of values that drive the thinking and the actions of an organization and its people day in and day out. It is the foundation that creates the persona or brand of a business that becomes the natural behavior internally and that is exuded externally.

Too often, people equate *culture* with casual Fridays, "party" workplaces, or endless corporate freebies. True culture, however, is pervasive and intentional. It is those living values that mold everything a company and its employees do, their internal processes and procedures, and their interactions with customers and communities, and corporate bottom lines.

Everyone makes financial and business decisions based on an organization's culture. If a company makes or provides a good product; if customers like how an individual or a company does business—their honesty, integrity, and dependability; if they appreciate the customer service; if processes are smooth and simple—all of this is a part of the company's conscious culture.

Culture, too, makes the difference between an organization that thrives through good and bad economic times, and one that struggles.

This book is your front-row seat to building and perpetuating a successful culture in any business, no matter its size or the competition. When you get the culture right, your company will succeed. You'll hire the right people. You'll invest in them—it's not about spending extra cash. You and your employees will share common values. You'll communicate with good intentions. And together, you'll move toward a common vision and mission—your company's long-term success.

Culture comes from the top. If the leadership of a company gets it—if they understand the importance of positive values and how to implement them—that values-based culture emanates outward and downward in terms of a company and its people's thoughts, actions, policies, procedures, and products or services.

Culture isn't some vague concept. It actually translates into dollars and cents at the bottom line. Companies with strong values-based cultures have nearly twice the annualized returns compared with the Standard & Poor's (S&P) 500,[1] according to research by Russell Investments (www. RussellInvestments.com) for the Great Place to Work Institute®.

The Institute produces the annual CNN Money/Fortune Best Companies to Work For list.

Plenty of people regularly talk about culture and values, yet, based on the few companies that get it right, most miss the mark on implementation.

After nearly three decades as Human Resources/Culture and Talent leader at some of the world's top corporations and alongside outstanding leaders, I have been fortunate to gain a firsthand perspective on how the best of the best develop and perpetuate a real values-based culture. To create that culture requires an understanding of the bottom-line value of culture, what's necessary to build high-performance cultures, the nuances of what works and what doesn't, and how to overcome the obstacles. I've learned all that and more working with teams at various companies, including:

*Allscripts Healthcare Solutions, where as Executive Vice President of Culture and Talent, the focus was on people integration as the company grew from 2,000 to 7,000 employees and revenues jumped from $548.4 million to $1.444 billion.

*Cisco Systems, where as Vice President of Human Resources, our teams oversaw the hiring and culture integration of tens of thousands of new hires as the company's revenues jumped from $2.2 billion to more than $40 billion.

*Nortel in human resources leadership roles, and as an independent consultant with other leading companies, the focus has always been on culture, organization, and leadership development.

My roles include regular collaboration on culture with many of today's extraordinary leaders, too. A few of these individuals include

*John Chambers, Executive Chairman of Cisco, a master at understanding how long-term success depends on a culture of collaboration and communication;

*Glen Tullman, CEO Livongo Health, venture capitalist and former CEO of Allscripts, an expert on the link between a dynamic company culture and exceptional performance;

*Nido Qubein, PhD., President of High Point University, and a proponent of communications in creating a positive culture;

*Lars Bjork, CEO of high-tech giant Qlik, who realizes that an accessible management style can drive a positive culture.

*Brad Wilson, CEO of Blue Cross Blue Shield of North Carolina (BCBSNC), with his unparalleled recognition of the connection between nurturing a healthy and happy workforce, and a culture of success.

With their companies, these people make it a priority to create great places to work and learn—essential ingredients in developing a successful culture in any business.

In these pages, I'll share my experiences and insights with these and other extraordinary leaders and their companies. You'll learn about the passion and persistence required to create a values-based culture in your company. You'll see how successful companies build these cultures despite stiff competition and up and down economies. You'll also see in action the values that matter and make a difference in your company's ability to sustain long-term growth.

Too often, businesses and their leaders tell me that changing a company's culture is too overwhelming or too expensive. Yet creating the right culture doesn't have to be either. This is culture as a way of life, not simply free coffee and casual Fridays. This is about how your organization—whether it's a small corner business or a global conglomerate—can operate with integrity. That doesn't take extra money. Neither does living and working within your stated values as opposed to only paying them lip service.

Over the years, I have helped develop an approach to building a successful business culture that revolves around implementing values common to all long-term successful companies. The seven essential values that are a part of most successful company cultures include

- *integrity and respect,*
- *innovation,*
- *communication and collaboration,*
- *customer success,*
- *giveback/social responsibility*
- *learning and education, and*
- *leaders who drive operational excellence net extraordinary results.*

In this book, I'll show you how each value can make a difference for your company and what it takes to implement these values. With the help of the 7 Points to Culture system for success, you'll know what to do and how to do it. I'll include examples of successful and not-so-successful cultures at various companies and in different situations. I'll provide explanations of how and why an approach or action did or did not succeed, and tips on how to do it better.

Each chapter will include stories and practical advice, as well as related exercises and assessments to help you identify company and personal strengths and weaknesses, and determine where you are on the path to creating a positive culture in your organization. There's an accompanying online workbook, too, that you can access by visiting www.DianeKAdams. com, and clicking on the icon, "It Takes More than Casual Fridays and Free Coffee."

My hope is that the stories and insights in this book will at times make you laugh or even think, "You've got to be kidding." But most important, I hope they'll inspire you with the courage and knowledge to take action and build a culture in your company that's true to your values. The path to success isn't easy. But few things worth doing ever are.

PART I

Values Matter

CHAPTER 1

Culture: Why You Should Care

People don't care how much you know until they know how much you care.

—*Diane K. Adams*

Culture is the game changer in work and in life. It's the great differentiator in success or the lack thereof. Get it right and an organization thrives. Miss the mark and you lose.

When I first started in the field of human resources more than 25 years ago, a struggling manufacturing organization's C-suite brought me in to fix what they assumed was a simple matter of employees disgruntled with their leadership—even though the company paid competitive wages, absenteeism was up, and plant production had dropped 20 percent. The executive team thought a human resources specialist could shore up morale and hopefully in turn bring production back to normal levels. They warned me, though, that the plant managers could be "difficult."

I walked into the plant the first day and quickly realized "difficult" was an understatement. The two longtime comanagers were tyrants who ruled as dictators. The plant operated with a culture of fear. I initially thought that if I could help the employees better cope in a culture of intimidation and fear, the business could turn around. I also tried to coach the plant's leaders to change their management approach to embrace a more motivational style that valued employees. After four months of my trying, though, they refused to listen. They simply became more defensive and angry that I would even suggest that they operate their plant any differently. One day I was off-site on company business when one of the comanagers called and told me "to get my (bleep) back to the plant because," he informed me, "when you're working for me, you ask permission before leaving this building." That was my turning point. Culture comes from the top. I realized plant management had to change for the company to change. The solution became clear. I went back to the C-suite executives who had brought me in and told them that no amount of strategic planning or actions would make any difference in the company's bottom line without a seismic change in the culture, starting with removing the tyrannical managers.

Fortunately, the executives believed that my assessment was correct, and within days they let the managers go. Almost immediately employee morale increased. The company brought in new leaders who worked to change the once-crippling culture. The executive team empowered the new leaders to change their culture and grow their teams, which inevitably grew their business. The new leaders provided clear direction. Teams were recognized and rewarded, and the company invested in leadership and employee development. Within a year, the plant's finances turned around, and eventually they went on to exceed expectations.

Never underestimate the value of feeling valued, whether you're on the assembly line or you're a CEO of a Fortune 500 company.

Though my time at the plant was hard, I wouldn't have traded the experience for anything. I now understood that culture really does trump strategy.

What Is Culture?

Culture is the set of clear values that drive the thinking, actions, attitudes, and guidelines of an organization and its people day in and day out. It's a way of life. Companies have unique cultures—and so do families, schools, churches, and favorite sports teams.

Culture affects organizations, their employees, customers, and the communities they touch.

The Differentiator

I've seen it time and again in my experience working with a variety of organizations. Get the culture right, and your organization will thrive. Get it wrong, and the company will struggle and ultimately fail.

Consider Sweden-based Qlik, today one of the world's fastest-growing companies in the business analytics space. Lars Bjork, now CEO, began as CFO, ranked as employee No. 35. But from the beginning, he recognized that the core to Qlik's long-term success lay in getting the culture right.

To that end, he and the company's other employees spent hours together defining the values they wanted to see come alive in every employee and for Qlik. They not only communicated those values clearly and consistently but also set up Qlik Academy—an employee orientation program held in Sweden that's designed to reinforce in employees the company's values from Day 1. All 2,100 of Qlik's current employees have attended.

Flying everyone to Sweden for the orientation is a big expense. But, says Lars, the impact of everyone understanding clearly the company's values and expectations is worth the investment. He's always reminding me, "happy people, happy customers, happy finances…in that order."

Size Doesn't Matter When It Comes to Culture

On a smaller scale, despite the housing crisis that's gripped the country and crippled the businesses of many Realtors™ over the last several years, I've watched Rachel Kendall Realty soar. Today, the eastern North Carolina (Triangle area) affiliate of Keller Williams Realty is one of the top Realtors in that region, even though it has just 14 people. In its six short years in business, the company has climbed to among the top in the Raleigh and Triangle region of the state.[1]

Team Effort. Time after time, clients, former clients, and employees point to the Kendall culture of transparency and personal care and concern as reasons for its success. It's also because Rachel is intentional about creating a culture in which her team excels. Her team will tell you how their boss is their mentor, how she takes them with her on appointments, and how she brings them together to celebrate their wins in work and in life.

It's a culture that's led to some amazing statistics—96 percent of the company's business comes from referrals.

I recently turned to Rachel's firm in a search for a home for a family member. After our appointment on July 5, the Realtor told me, she was headed to a company day-after-Fourth-of-July party at Rachel's home. What a great personal way to reinforce a positive and caring culture at the firm.

When you say "culture," people look at you like a deer in headlights, says Kendall, a former schoolteacher and fitness guru turned real estate broker. But she points to her company's success as being a direct result of its culture.

Guiding Principles. That culture is more than free lunches on Wednesdays at Rachel Kendall Realty's business meetings. "Culture is the guiding premise on everything that we do," says Rachel. "If we put culture first and we truly live and work and conduct ourselves based on the guiding principles we created...people will be treated well; people will know we care; people will want to do business with us...and people will want to be on our team. Good energy attracts good energy.

"If you put people first really and truly, and you have a system [a culture], you will always be successful. The problem in business, especially in this business [real estate], is that people put money first. To those people, I say, 'I hope you enjoyed the transaction because your business is not going to grow' because you don't have any culture."

A Powerful Effect. Rachel is on point. Do you ever wonder why companies like Cisco, Google, SAS, and Disney are successful year after year? Or why retailers like Zappos.com, Costco, and CarMax always get great press?

They are intentional and pervasive about culture. They define their values—the foundation for their culture—from the beginning. Yes, these companies pay wages that compare favorably with those in their industry, but that's standard operating procedure. They differentiate themselves because they care about creating extraordinary and memorable experiences for their constituents—employees, customers, and partners.

Personal Connections. At Cisco Systems, with a worldwide employment of 70,000, former CEO and now Executive Chairman John Chambers always personally called any employee who experienced a serious illness or tragedy to offer his support and that of the company or team.

So did Glen Tullman, during his tenure as the CEO of Allscripts Healthcare Solutions. While I was at Allscripts, one day Glen and I were in an important meeting of company leaders. I received a call that an employee's son in the military had been severely injured by a roadside bomb in Afghanistan. Sadly, he had lost both of his legs. Glen and I excused ourselves from the meeting, immediately contacted the employee—the soldier's mother—and left to visit her and her family to find out how we could help. Later, after Nathan Rimpf, the injured soldier, was transferred to a military hospital in Washington, DC,

Glen flew there several times to visit him. At the time, Allscripts had 7,000 employees.

That's a culture of caring deeply for your employees. And it extended beyond the C-suite. The injured soldier's mother, Cindy, spent four months by her son's side, all the while her fellow workers voluntarily picked up the slack to allow her the freedom to be with her son. Cindy's coworkers even sold "Nathan Rimpf" wristbands to raise money to help with expenses. Glen still wears the wristband three years later.

I will always remember the day my daughter Danielle was diagnosed with type 1 diabetes. At the time, she was four years old, and I was with Cisco. Then-CEO Chambers and Rick Justice, who led the company's worldwide sales team of thousands of employees, were the first two people to call and check on her (and me) at the hospital.

Beyond the calls, John later donated Cisco technology to the Juvenile Diabetes Research Foundation, which works to accelerate the finding of a cure for diabetes. Rick invested personally, too, with understanding and support. He gave me total flexibility in my job so that I could make Danielle's health a priority. With a company that cared that much, I wanted more than ever to deliver our best. My team helped the company produce another phenomenal year of growth.

Big or Small

Caring for your employees isn't only standard procedure at top-performing global giants with standout cultures, either. Small, unheralded companies embrace it as a way of life, too.

My favorite vice is butter pecan ice cream. I've been known to eat it at all hours of the day and night, and around the globe. As you can imagine, I'm always looking for a better scoop, too. That was until I found Lumpy's. This North Carolina small-and-growing ice cream producer has the freshest, healthiest, and best-tasting butter pecan I've ever consumed.

And, making the product even better, Lumpy's has a best-culture to match. Not only does owner Buck Buchanan care about producing spectacular ice cream, he also cares about his employees, too—all 20 of them at the height of the season. One of those employees lost a loved one and worried she couldn't attend the funeral for financial reasons. Buchanan stepped in and picked up the tab, while fellow Lumpy's employees pitched in work-wise to make up for the employee's absence.

Who wouldn't go the extra mile for companies and their people who care like that? Customers do the same in terms of their financial support. Both Allscripts and Cisco have survived and thrived amid intense economic swings as well as strong competition. Lumpy's business began and thrived mostly amid a recession.

Financial Incentive

Those "extra miles" turn into extraordinary results. Analysis from Russell Investments shows that historically companies with positive values-based cultures, as measured by the publicly listed companies on the CNN Money/Fortune Best Companies to Work For annual list, have tended to outperform the US stock market. Mark Soupiset, director of corporate communications for Russell, explained that annually his company looks at the publicly traded companies in the Best list and measures their performance against that of the Russell 3000 Index and the Standard & Poor's (S&P) 500 Index. The Best Companies to Work For list identifies the best places to work based on a variety of factors that relate to a positive values-based company culture, including employee feedback.

WHY CULTURE MATTERS: THE BOTTOM LINE
(1998/Q1–2014/Q4)

Russell Investments looked at the returns of the publicly listed companies on the CNN Money/Fortune Best Companies to Work For annual list and compared them to the returns of the general stock market over time as measured by the Russell 3000 and the Standard & Poor's (S&P) 500 indexes.

The Details:

- *Portfolio A invests equal dollar amounts at the beginning of 1998 in the stock of each of the publicly traded companies in the "Best 100." The portfolio is liquidated at the end of 1998, with the proceeds then invested in the 1999 list. The same liquidation and purchase process continues through 2014.*

- *Portfolio B invests equal dollar amounts at the beginning of 1998 in the stock of each of the publicly traded companies in the "Best 100" and holds these through 2014.*

Table 1.1 The results

	Portfolio A	Portfolio B	Russell 3000	S&P 500
Annualized return:	11.07%	12.71%	6.76%	6.48%
Cumulative Return:	584.0%	664.2%	204.0%	190.7%

Source: ©Russell Investments (www.Russell.com)

Russell analysis also found that publicly traded companies on the CNN Money/Fortune Great Place to Work For list saw a more than 664 percent increase in their cumulative stock performance 1998 to 2014 That compares with a 204 percent increase for Russell 3000 companies and only 190.7 for the S&P 500.

BUSINESS RESULTS OF ENGAGEMENT

Companies save big bucks when their employees are engaged. Consider these concrete results of engaged employees, according to a Society of Human Resources Management report sponsored by Randstad:

At Molson Coors, the beverage company:

- *Highly engaged employees were five times less likely than nonengaged employees to have a safety incident and seven times less likely to experience a lost-time safety incident.*
- *Stronger employee engagement saved the company more than $1.7 million in safety costs in one year.*

At Caterpillar, the construction-equipment maker:

- *Increased employee engagement led to less attrition, absenteeism, and overtime at one European plant, and a plant savings of $8.8 million annually.*
- *The same plants saw a $2 million increase in profits.*
- *Increased employee engagement netted a 34 percent increase in satisfied customers at a start-up plant.*

Source: Society of Human Resource Management (www.shrm.org)[2]

Beyond the Money

That kind of sustainably better performance also in part relates to happier employees. That happiness comes not from costly freebies and perks, and not even necessarily the from highest salaries. It comes from values-based cultures that create connected and committed—highly engaged—employees. Worldwide, though, only one in eight employees is fully engaged in his or her work—truly committed to his or her job and likely to make positive contributions, according to Gallup research.[3] That means 87 percent of employees in the world aren't engaged in their jobs, aren't producing at their best, and are unnecessarily costing their companies tens of millions of billions of dollars every year.

THE CASE FOR CULTURE

Why does culture matter to your bottom line? Consider some of the results from recent studies and reports that examine the importance of employee engagement:

Employees who are committed to their jobs

- work 57 percent harder on the job;*
- are 87 percent less likely to resign, compared with disengaged employees;*
- feel satisfaction with their work;†

- take pride in their organization;[†]
- enjoy and believe in their work;[†]
- understand the link between their job and the organization's mission;[†]
- feel valued by their employer;[†]
- fully commit to their employer and to their role;[†]
- exert extra effort to contribute to business success.[†]

*Corporate Executive Board's Corporate Leadership Council[4]
[†] Society of Human Resources Management[5]

Stellar Experiences

One of my favorite examples of a company that doesn't pay the highest salaries—its salaries reflect the industry median instead—but attracts and retains its employees because of its culture is North Carolina-based tech giant SAS. In fact, in an industry in which the average employee turnover is 15 percent annually, SAS has barely 4 percent turnover. People love to work there. The company is No. 2 on the 2014 CNN Money/Fortune Best Place to Work For list for a reason. The company has the work/life balance figured out.

When it's working well, a culture provides an environment in which employees are compensated fairly—where they enjoy their work, their colleagues, their work environment, and they have ample opportunity to grow professionally and personally. Companies in return experience better bottom lines.

Growing Bottom Lines

Remember that struggling manufacturer with its tyrannical comanagers that I talked about earlier in the chapter—the one that experienced a 20 percent drop in production by the time the comanagers were let go? Under new management and less than a year later, the plant's positive culture had been restored, production had returned to normal and, in fact, it went on to exceed expectations.

Commitment to Values. When I joined Allscripts to lead its Culture and Talent organization, the company had $500 million in revenues. Within three years and with management's strong commitment to its values-based culture, those revenues tripled to nearly $1.44 billion.

A big part of that commitment included establishing what we called CLEAR values. The CLEAR acronym represented Client success, Leadership, Extraordinary people, Aspire, and Results. In practice, that meant the company's success began with putting the client's needs first, and with the help of our extraordinary people, we were able to create outstanding results.

For Allscripts, success was about more than paying competitive salaries. We invested in people through ongoing learning opportunities. To make the learning more fun, we even held contests and awarded prizes to the first 25 people who completed training programs.

Recognition and Celebration. Recognition was a huge part of the culture. At all-hands meetings—we called them town hall meetings—leaders would recognize customer and employee successes to further reinforce extraordinary performance.

We made celebrating success part of the culture. One year, our customer support team had to work hard through the New Year's holiday because of a new product rollout. No problem, though. We celebrated New Year's Eve in February with our customer support team. They loved it!

The Human Factor

So why is it so hard to get the culture right? Because we are human. And with that comes each person's own experiences, prejudices, varying degrees of trust, and agendas. We too often think about *me* instead of *we*.

As Qlik CEO Bjork often says, "We talk too much and listen too little." And, too often companies think of culture as the *soft stuff* versus the *real and hard* stuff that impacts the bottom line.

CULTURE COUNTS

Company leaders overwhelmingly agree that culture is the major competitive differentiator, yet few go on to create a winning culture, according to research from Bain & Company:

- *68 percent believe their culture is a competitive advantage.*
- *76 percent believe a culture can be changed.*

- *65 percent know they need to change their company's culture.*
- *81 percent say that an organization without a high-performance culture is doomed to mediocrity.*
- *Less than 10 percent succeed in building that high-performance culture.*

*A Bain survey of 365 companies in Europe, Asia, and North America (www. Bain.com)[6]

Put everyone in the same room, and they will work things out, right? I wish it were that easy. But what I can say is that there is a common approach you can take to build an extraordinary culture in your business.

It starts with integrity and values, and living those values on the inside and the outside.

Pervasive and Intentional

In 1978, Ben Cohen and Jerry Greenfield opened an ice cream shop in a renovated gas station in Burlington, Vermont. What mattered most to them back then, the duo told me many years later, was to make a good product, build a company with great service, and live their values. Those values, they told me, meant being socially responsible and giving back to the community.

In those early years, the idea of ever becoming international giants in the ice cream business definitely wasn't on Ben or Jerry's agenda. But, get the culture right and the rest takes care of itself. What mattered to the committed and innovative pair instead was running their business—no matter how small at the time—with their positive values. It wasn't until years later that Ben and Jerry admitted to me that they now recognized the real impact their approach to culture could and did have on their business.

Literally zillions of scoops, pints, and quarts of Chocolate Chip Cookie Dough, Cherry Garcia®, and many other flavors later is Ben and Jerry's ice cream history. Ben and Jerry sold their company to international giant Unilever in 2000. By then, the company's culture was ingrained, as was its persona and its brand. Today, more than two decades later, the keystones of good product, social responsibility, and more remain. Unilever continues to support Ben & Jerry's founding values: economic and social justice, environmental restoration, and peace through understanding, and to support Vermont communities. Ben & Jerry's still is a Vermont corporation. The company continues to donate product to nonprofits and community groups, and contributions made via the employee-led Ben & Jerry's Foundation in 2012 totaled $1.8 million.[7]

Culture Ambassadors

At Allscripts, to disseminate and perpetuate the company's team culture, we made sure every company location globally had a "culture ambassador" on the team. These were individuals who thoroughly understood all aspects of the company's culture and were responsible for helping others understand it, too.

A big part of the culture ambassador's job was to foster relationships and camaraderie that in turn accelerated workplace and bottom-line results. That meant making the workplace fun, too.

Sporting your favorite team's jersey in the office on the Friday before the Super Bowl, for example, may sound like a waste of company time and effort to some people. But culture ambassadors and Allscripts' culture-wise leadership knew better. This and other similar activities can foster better communications and relationships between people—important aspects of a collaborative and successful workplace.

A potluck lunch or dinner once a month or so can do the same thing, especially in smaller companies. These kinds of participatory activities can help create excitement, energize teams, and add to the collaboration and creativity among employees. A culture ambassador or designee can help make it happen.

(A word of caution when it comes to fun: fun is created much more easily and naturally when people first feel that their basic needs like fair compensation and benefits are being met.)

The Importance of Relationships

The bottom line is that people who talk and get to know each other in a casual setting often work better together to solve business problems. It's a way to develop relationships, interactions, and communications among employees, across departments, and across all levels of a company.

After all, when people are willing to talk with each other, it's much easier to sit down and work through solving problems and issues—no matter how difficult.

It's Not So Overwhelming

So often people tell me they're overwhelmed by even the idea of changing a company's culture. They tell me it's too big and too expensive even to think about. But to create a positive culture is neither of those things. It's not about paying the highest salaries, throwing lavish parties, or providing endless perks.

The Cost of Integrity and Values

Living and acting with integrity doesn't take extra cash. Neither does volunteering in the community or living and working within your stated values as opposed to only paying them lip service.

These are all crucial aspects of a true values-based culture.

You Can't Afford Not to Think Culture

Sepideh (Sepi) Saidi has a message for companies and their leaders who think culture is too expensive. She has the same words for those who say they're too busy to bother with it. Sepi is the president and founder of SEPI Engineering, one of the largest private full-service engineering firms in North Carolina, with more than 150 employees across the state.

"If you don't pay attention to culture, you won't have a payroll to worry about. It's so important, especially if you want to grow your company," she says.

As the leader of a company, it's about the values you truly believe in, extending those values to your company's culture and to how you interact with clients. Saidi told me, "I have worked with folks who are saying the right things, but they aren't doing the right things."

Sepi truly understands how culture makes the difference. Ask her employees and her clients, and they'll tell you how much they like working with her because of her positive values that extend to how she operates her business. Those values range from showing honesty and integrity to encouraging open communications and collaboration, treating employees as assets, supporting community giveback, helping her customers succeed, and more.

Employees say they especially like that Sepi encourages everyone to share ideas and to listen. Every employee's voice counts and so do those of her clients. She truly lives her company's values-based culture. The company attracts top engineering talent, too, not because it pays top wages—it doesn't—but because of its strong culture.

Sepi encourages others to do well, Marissa Mansfield, SEPI human resources manager, told me. And that's a culture that makes a difference. "I've worked for other engineering firms. But (unlike other firms) Sepi encourages people to do well and succeed. A lot of what we focus on here is, if someone needs training, we give it to them. If someone needs help with something, we help. We want you to succeed with the company."

That's culture as the game changer for companies, their people, and their clients.

Culture Creates the Difference

A values-based culture demands that a company and its leadership make an intentional commitment to those values and have the courage to do what's necessary to live those values.

Sweet Success for a Small Business

Earlier I talked about my favorite ice cream shop, Lumpy's with its great ice cream and great culture. Lumpy's enthusiastic owner, Buchanan, cares about creating healthy ice cream, about giving back to his community, and about making people smile. He's been that way since trading his job teaching culinary classes to start the business out of a shed in the backyard of his Raleigh, North Carolina, home in 2001. Buchanan opted to pursue his passion over job security.

Culture is everything to Buchanan. "I love what I do as being that one person who can lift your spirit up when you know you're having a bad day," says Buchanan on a YouTube video for a 2012 television commercial.[8]

Walk into Lumpy's: everyone is upbeat. Talk to Buchanan or check out his website. Personal commitment and high values are paramount. They're evident in all aspects of what the growing company and its people do. On a recent gray January day, Lumpy's offered this Facebook post to its loyal fans:

"It's kind of cold and overcast outside but at Lumpy's Ice Cream it is complementary day. Stop by to get a scoop and an ego-inflating complement day"

Caring is simply a part of Lumpy's. It's the echo of what Southwest Airline's Herb Kelleher says—"Culture is what people do when no one is looking."[9] And it's being practiced by a small company.

Buchanan's values extend to how he treats his employees, too. It's family first, he says, and is evidenced by the story earlier in the chapter about how he and his Lumpy's team stepped up when another employee experienced a family tragedy. "Nobody really works for us. They work with us," the small business owner adds.

That kind of values-based culture rubs off on Lumpy's customers. Pay it forward happens all the time. A customer will come in, pay his or her bill, and leave an extra $10 to pay for the next person's ice cream.

As Lumpy's culture has spread, so has the company's success despite the recession. The company began with its shed production facility, one ice cream cart, and a pickup truck for distribution of just 30 to 60 gallons of product a week. Today, Lumpy's has three delivery trucks, a distribution trailer, five ice cream carts, and its retail outlet that together sell a total of 200 to 260 gallons of product a week. Lumpy's is served at local and regional upscale restaurants, and is available in retail stores, too.

Culture proves to be the catalyst for ongoing success.

Values Drive Culture

When I first met Sepi, she was on a podium addressing the Raleigh (North Carolina) Chamber of Commerce as its president. She was a confidant, poised, and powerful woman, yet she also was warm, gracious, and humble. Sepi later told me her story. An Iranian immigrant, she was sent to the United States by her parents as a teen to get an education. After graduating in engineering from North Carolina State University, she spent about a dozen years in highway design and traffic engineering with the North Carolina Department of Transportation before launching her own company.

From her company's beginnings in a back room of her home to today's highly touted success story, Sepi has remained true to her values—values like respect for others and the recognition and appreciation of the strengths each person brings to the company, along with social responsibility and giving back to the community. That's the foundation she's relied on to develop her company from zero to $20 million in a little more than a dozen years, much of that in recessionary times. As a member of her Advisory Board, I'm always impressed with her humility, her openness, and her wisdom.

Says Sepi, "One of the reasons I care so much about culture is that I care about how I feel about the company. I think it's wonderful on a Sunday night to actually look forward to going to work on Monday. I think when people feel happy about what they do, they do much more, and they give much more. It's not worth it to become the biggest engineering firm in the world without the culture. Even though someone may be able to get another $5,000 or $10,000 somewhere else, they come here (to my firm) because they feel a part of something much better, much more satisfying."

That satisfaction comes because Sepi really cares about honesty and integrity, collaboration and communication, and personal and professional success when it comes to her team members and her customers. She's truly committed to living all the positive values that create a great culture in a company.

Talk to her current employees, and it's the same story. It's about Sepi's honesty and integrity, her willingness to listen to others' ideas and opinions and to work as a team, all of which drives the company's meteoric success.

The Bottom Line

With the right culture in place, we hire the right people. We invest in them. We share common values. We communicate with good intentions. And we always move toward a common vision and mission.

The enterprise wins. And so does the individual.

Having Doubts about Culture?

If you're still not convinced a company's culture makes a difference, try this simple exercise the next time you're out. When you're at a company or in a store, talk to the employees. Ask them about their jobs, whether they enjoy them, and why or why not. Do they like working for the company, why or why not?

I promise you'll be surprised by the responses. The best businesses and the most successful ones likely will have the happiest and the most helpful employees.

Even though I know culture changes things, I still always ask these kinds of questions wherever I go. The responses still amaze me.

Not long ago I was shopping for a car. I walked into a CarMax store, introduced myself, and asked to speak to a salesperson. Shortly a sales associate came up, introduced herself, and we began chatting. I asked her if she liked working there. I had no idea at the time that CarMax repeatedly ranks on the CNN Money/Fortune Top 100 Best Places to Work list, or that CarMax actually rewards its employees with financial incentives to really live the company's culture as a way of life.

Without hesitation, the sales associate gushed about her company and its fabulous culture. As a single mom with a challenged daughter, she said she could not have thrived here without her CarMax "family" that's grounded in teamwork and inclusion. "Everyone has your back and everyone helps each other. My daughter has thrived, too," she said, "because I came to a company that believes in me, provides opportunities, and is an environment in which everyone supports each other."

Culture Check/The Basics

The right culture *can* make a difference for your company and your life, too. To do so demands honest and straightforward assessments.

As proven, successful companies do, you must first define the culture you have and then what you would like it to be. It's time to address the issues, and ask the right questions.

Questions that need to be answered include

- *What is our culture today?*
- *What do we want it to be in the future?*
- *What are the values that are most important to us as a company and as individuals?*
- *Do we consistently communicate these values in all that we say and do?*
- *How can we incorporate these values into everything we do as a company?*
- *Do we as a company, as leaders, and as employees, truly live these values?*
- *How does this values-based culture drive our success as a company and as individuals?*
- *How are we helping our customers succeed?*
- *What are we doing right today?*
- *What aren't we doing right, and how can we change that?*

These aren't just questions for you, but for your peers, teams, and leadership. Remember, it's about open and honest communications.

There aren't any right or wrong answers. Not everyone's answer will be the same, either, because every organization has its own culture, its own unique persona.

But your answers to the above questions can help you build the foundation for your own positive culture in your organization and in your life.

Next, ask the following questions and be honest in your answers. Again, they're questions for you, your peers, and even your leaders. The answers will provide a window into how better to develop your company's culture and in turn help ensure better bottom lines and sustained growth in the process.

- *Would you recommend this company to others as a good place to work? Why or why not?*
- *Are your team members proud to work for the company? Why or why not?*

In a culture that fosters values-based excellence, the answer to both questions above should be an unequivocal and resounding "yes." If the answers to either or both are "no," don't be discouraged. Be energized to make a difference and take action.

Now assume for a minute that one of your employees has a son in the military and that he has been deployed. You're in an important business meeting, and you just received word that the son was critically injured in a roadside bomb explosion.

Which of the following describes how you would react to your employee's tragedy?

1. *I would tell an assistant to send a condolence note immediately.*
2. *I would try to remember to offer my condolences after the meeting.*
3. *I would shrug my shoulders, and move on.*
4. *I would drop everything and make a personal visit to the employee to see how I could help.*

No matter how big or small your company, people don't care how much you know until they know how much you care. And truly caring people become truly caring employees personally and professionally.

CHAPTER 2

Are You Living a Double Life?

Culture is everything when it's right.

—*Diane K. Adams*

Values are the cornerstones to a successful, sustainable company culture. Yet most organizations only talk about values. Only the best companies are willing to do what's necessary to live them in everything the company and its people and leaders say and do.

Rhetoric versus Reality

Big companies often think fancy dinners, over-the-top celebrations, or lavish gifts are enough to create a great culture. Free day care, on-site food, and gym memberships are other approaches companies often try. It takes more than that to create a culture built on strong values that will sustain growth over the long haul.

The Slave Driver

Early in my human resources (HR) career, I spent a number of years with a large telecommunications provider, a one-time industry giant that's now defunct. The company constantly talked about how it cared about its employees and did plenty of things right. I actually made videos for the company that talked about flexibility in the workplace, too. Sounds good. The reality, however, was something else.

There was no workplace flexibility. I had to be at the office 12 to 15 hours a day, and three to four weekends a month. At the time, I had two children, then ages 4 and 6. I still remember the final straw that made me say, "Time to walk away!"

One Friday afternoon, the executive who headed research and development called me into his office at 6 p.m. He said he wanted to explain a number of things I had to get done that weekend. It was the same Friday that my son was "graduating" from pre-school. By the time the executive finished his list of to-dos, I ran out of the office and down the ramp, jumped into my car, and tore over to the preschool. Tears streamed down my face. I was so worried that I would miss my son's graduation.

The company seemed to care only about my getting the job done, and that's when I decided, no more. I made it to the graduation ceremony, but after that I began making plans to leave the company. Its values—the culture—simply didn't match my own. I could no longer reconcile the rhetoric with the reality.

A Better Way

Contrast that experience with what happened while I worked for Cisco. Not long after I joined California-based Cisco, my father, who lived in Raleigh, NC, developed cancer. As I've mentioned, ours is a close-knit family. I knew I needed to be with my parents.

I told my bosses at Cisco the situation, and that I needed to move back to Raleigh. They told me, "No problem. We trust you to get the job done no matter where you live."

And I did!

More Talk

One-time US energy giant Enron had a nice-sounding values statement with words like integrity, communication, respect, and excellence. The words were chiseled in marble on the interior walls of the lobby in the company's massive Houston headquarters.

It was the 1990s, and Enron was the darling of Wall Street. The company threw lavish parties. Its executives raked in huge bonuses, led over-the-top lifestyles, and enjoyed all the perks of success. But it was the ultimate case of a company with a double life. In reality, Enron's finances proved something very different when the walls of power tumbled down.

Amid scandal, the company declared bankruptcy in 2001. Coupled with the subsequent fallout, tens of thousands of workers, shareholders, and retirees lost billions of dollars. Company executives were convicted of crimes ranging from fraud and money laundering, to conspiracy and insider training. Once among the world's accounting powerhouses, Arthur Andersen, Enron's auditor, was left in ruins.[1]

You Are Your Values

EOG Resources is a sharp contrast to Enron. The company was spun off from Enron as Enron Oil and Gas prior to the bankruptcy. The new company, which later changed its name to EOG, apparently believed in Enron's original chiseled-in-stone high values. Consistently, the company appears on the CNNMoney/Forbes annual 100 Best Companies to Work For list. Its employees point to the company's strong culture as a big reason for this.

That culture pays big financial dividends for the company and its shareholders, too. EOG shares have returned more than 650 percent over the last decade, more than any other sizable US oil company, according to *Forbes* reports last year.[2]

Beyond the Perks

Harvard researchers, studying the impact of corporate culture on sustainability and performance, found that values-based cultures like that at EOG do make a difference in a company's success. Successful companies are those that look beyond the traditional model of corporate profits. That traditional model ignores social and environmental issues and responsibilities—both associated with a positive values-based culture.

Successful companies instead invest heavily in relationships with employees and customers, research shows.[3]

Happier—more engaged—employees, after all, mean better bottom lines. How much better? In the retail sector, for example, happy employees take 15 fewer sick days a year. They generate more in earnings, too—an additional $21 per square foot of space, according to Gallup research.[4]

Values Play a Role in Every Action and Reaction

To be successful, a culture and the values associated with it must be pervasive. They must resonate from leaders to employees in everything that's said and done in a company. They are the foundation for every goal that's laid out, every strategy to achieve those goals, and in every process, procedure, and interaction internally with employees and externally with customers and the community.

Without that broad buy-in—that absolute alignment to embrace the stated values—a company's culture won't succeed long term. The stated values at Enron didn't align with the company's actions. The company professed one set of values to the public, while its executives were committed to another, less honorable reality that revolved around fast profits, fast living, and disregard for rules, regulations, honesty, and integrity.

In contrast, at EOG the company's positive values and its actions align with the resulting dramatic and long-term positive financial results and in spite of difficult external economics—a major recession.

Cultural Courage

If there's a roadblock to that alignment—perhaps an employee or leader unwilling to accept the values—a company's leaders must be willing to recognize the problem and take action. This happens all the time. An employee or a team leader refuses to accept a company's stated value—an all-inclusive workplace, for example—rejects attempts at training and education, and simply continues with his or her prejudices.

Company leaders must stand up for the stated value and show what I call cultural courage.

At winning companies, you'll find that kind of long-term commitment to do what's right and necessary to adhere to the companies' values.

Brand at Risk

Cultural courage isn't always easy, but it's essential. Your company's reputation and brand are on the line. That's a risk no company can afford to take today if it wants to remain competitive.

Think of a successful business as a well-oiled machine made up of many gears. When one cog in one gear in the machine is off, the entire machine locks up. The same is true of your business. If each person or department is responsible for completing a task in order to finish a job, if one person or department falls short, the job doesn't get done.

Leaders must step up and make the hard decisions to weed out those cogs or those individuals who aren't culture matches. Otherwise, no matter what you do, your company can't be as successful long term.

Tough Job

Years ago I worked with a company in which the top bosses knew the importance of total buy-in to the company's culture. It included values like Collaboration, Open Communication, and Integrity and Respect. Unfortunately, though, one long-time leader—the head of customer support—balked.

Routinely, this long-time leader would fly into fits of rage he leveled at one or another of his team members. It was frightening, especially if you were the one singled out for the attack. When he lost his temper, his face flushed crimson. The longer the profanity-laced tirade continued, the darker red his face became. Inevitably the rants included the threat of job loss, too.

Usually the tantrum was triggered by an employee who had escalated a customer complaint. That meant the employee, working to resolve the issue, had brought in support from outside the department. The leader rationalized that his behavior was warranted because any time a problem escalated beyond his team that reflected negatively on him.

Misguided Actions. The reality, however, was that in escalating the complaints, customer support employees were doing what was necessary for resolution. The real problem lay in bugs in the company's software. That meant the quicker outside team members—specifically research and development experts—could get involved and fix the problems, the faster the complaints could be resolved satisfactorily. The out-of-control boss knew that, too.

But instead of recognizing the complexity of the problems and bringing in other leaders to solve the bigger issue, this leader constantly leveled individual blame against his employees and let his anger take over.

Unacceptable Behavior. That type of behavior is unacceptable in the workplace in any situation, no matter how veteran an employee or how long a leader has held his or her position. Uncontrollable anger does not belong in any company culture.

People don't work at their best under a cloud of fear. Remember the manufacturing plant tyrants from chapter 1? With the tyrants in control and employees afraid for their jobs, plant production dropped dramatically. After the source of the fear—the tyrannical comanagers—were removed, production soared.

With the telecommunications company, its executives had tried reprimanding the veteran leader, but decided to overlook his tirades. They feared negative backlash if they tried to remove him. The fits and the subsequently unhappy employees, they rationalized, were an uncomfortable part of doing business.

Eventually, though, after several top employees came to me visibly shaken and worried about their jobs, management realized that the leader had to go. He simply and visibly did not represent the company's strong values.

Frightening Tirade. Tasked with the firing, I worried how the man might react. So I had security standing by outside the door when I called him into my office. Still, I was shocked by what ensued. When I explained to the individual that the company had decided to release him and the reasons why, he flew into a rage he directed at me. Of course he blamed the situation all on me.

It was early in my career, and as yet I had never encountered anyone who had that much anger bottled up and was so unwilling to accept any responsibility for his actions. Thankfully, though, with security's help, the man finally left the building.

A Footnote to the Affair. After the man was fired, customer complaints at the company actually decreased because his replacement, the new leader of customer support, understood the company's commitment to Collaboration, and worked with teams across departments to solve the root issues of customer complaints.

Culture Matching in Hiring

Instead of having to deal with the results of a poor culture match, as above, savvy companies try to hire upfront with culture matching in mind. This approach saves hassles, heartache, and hard cash. A culture mismatch can end up costing your company employee buyouts if warranted in a dismissal, the cost of lost business as a result of unhappy customers, and the added cost of rehiring and retraining replacements for culture mismatches.

Top companies often design their job interview questions to reflect the company's strong values and culture. If a candidate doesn't match, he or she is out, period. That's as it should be, no exceptions.

Recognizing the Mismatch. Over the last few years a large company has approached me to join its ranks. It's a prestigious company, yet it's not the right place for me.

The company obviously doesn't know it, but I do—I'm not a match for its culture. The company simply moves too slowly.

Remember, culture comes from the top. If top leadership rejects a major value in a culture, then you must have the cultural courage to step back and walk away, too.

The Values That Matter

Different values are important to different companies because every person and every company has unique goals and concerns. But all successful companies have identified those values that matter.

No One Size Fits All

At fast-growing software company Qlik, for example, the company is young and the industry is rapid fire in terms of change. As a result, we've identified Moving Fast as a key value for helping the company maintain its competitive advantage. The strategy to implement that value calls for Discover, Decide, Do—make quick decisions with input from the right individuals and the right data before taking action.

On the other hand, Zappos! (www.Zappos.com) as an online retailer has identified Customer Service as a value it needs to stay ahead. Therefore Moving Fast isn't a good fit as a value for Zappos!, but Deliver WOW through Service is.

Core Values

Based on my years of experience developing cultures, growing companies, and turning around businesses, I've learned that all long-term successful companies share nuances of the same seven essential values.

Those values include

- **Integrity and respect.** These companies foster an all-inclusive workplace.
- **Innovation.** Winning companies promote discovering new and better ways of thinking and of accomplishing goals.

- **Open communication and collaboration**. Success is a team effort; everyone is a contributor.
- **Customer success**. A company's success is a natural outgrowth of its customers' success.
- **Giveback/social responsibility**. It's the right thing to do, plus giving back to others fosters long-term loyalty through good and bad economic times.
- **Learning is your edge. Invest in your people**. Ongoing employee learning and education pay dividends because your employees' growth fuels your company's growth.
- **Leaders who drive operational excellence net extraordinary results**. Culture comes from the top, and so does operational excellence. Great leaders develop great companies with great cultures

With these values in place and integrated into your company's way of life, you and your company will succeed where others don't.

Spreading the Word

Successful companies develop different ways of understanding, promoting, and implementing their positive values—from education and training to rewards and recognition. Everyone must realize the company's culture and the values associated with it, why they're important, how they figure into a company's financial success, and how real implementation manifests itself in the workplace and space.

Methods. Allscripts had its *culture ambassadors,* the culture experts mentioned in the last chapter, who spread positivity about its culture. Modeling the right values—the opposite of the Enron experience—works, too.

So does reinforcing positive behaviors in the form of reward and/or recognition of those individuals whose actions uphold and personify a value.

The Allscripts Example

Allscripts' orientation and training included in-depth explanations of the company's culture and its strong values. Training was mandatory for leaders as well as employees, for new hires, and for those new to the company through acquisition. We believed—rightfully so—that our culture of high values and excellence distinguished us from our competitors in the health-care technology field.

Winning Talent. We attracted and retained top talent. Consistently, people told me they chose Allscripts because the company really cared—about them, about their contributions to the company, and about the community. They liked, too, that Allscripts had a purpose beyond profits.

Growth at Bottom Line. By emphasizing our positive values-based culture across all our internal and external interactions, we also created a working environment that allowed the company's performance to excel. Revenues soared from just over $500 million to nearly $1.5 billion in the same time frame.

Our people succeeded, too. Over the years, many have gone on to lead other prestigious successful companies or companies of their own.

CLEARly Important

To help promote our culture's values year-round, my team developed an internal marketing campaign: "CLEAR*ly a Great Place to Work*."

CLEAR was an acronym that represented traits associated with our values:

- Client Experience: Clients are always first.
- Leadership: Think, inspire, motivate, and communicate.
- Extraordinary People: Passionate, caring, and fun.
- Aspiration: Think different, think big.
- Results: Say and do.

Repeat Recognition. The CLEAR logo and discussions about the values associated with it became a regular fixture in all formal meetings. CLEAR wall posters were displayed in offices and hallways throughout the company and at all its locations as a constant reminder of Allscripts' values and how they should play into every company process, action, and communication.

Employee Recognition, Reward. At all-hands meetings, leaders also recognized employees and other leaders for specific actions that exemplify the company's stated values.

For example, I remember an instance in which a sales employee worked extremely hard to help a customer resolve an internal issue crucial to the customer's success. At the next Allscripts all-hands meeting, CEO Glen Tullman recognized that employee for his tireless work in helping his customer succeed. In pointing out that effort, Glen said it personified the Allscripts core value of Customer Success: a customer's success is our success. The customer's problem wasn't a direct link to Allscript's product, but it did make a big difference for the customer.

In addition to Glen's announcement, the employee's name and his or her accomplishment were posted on the company Intranet, and he or she received a small financial incentive—perhaps a gift card to a local coffee shop.

(If your company doesn't have an Intranet, a company bulletin board on a wall in the break room will work, too. It's about recognition.)

It's Not about Cost

Any company of any size can promote its culture through its values internally and externally.

Your company's approach doesn't have to be as complicated, costly, or complex and extensive as what we did at Allscripts. But it does take a conscious commitment to action.

Incentives for team members who excel can range from simple recognition among peers to financial incentives. Some suggestions for incentives include

- Small-denomination gift cards to local favorite hangouts, movie tickets, or even cash.
- Anything that includes an employee's family or friends can be a plus—a dinner for the employee's family or friends at a local restaurant, for example.

Remember, it's not necessarily the dollar amount; rather, it's the recognition of a job well done.

Overcoming the Instant-Return Approach

By now you, too, can begin to see the link between getting culture right and business success. With numbers and results so overwhelmingly favoring culture, you would think creating a positive culture would be a no-brainer for any company looking to succeed long term.

But it's not. Too many companies and their leaders still ignore or lose track of the value of culture in favor of what those Harvard researchers, mentioned above, refer to as the traditional model of corporate profits.

Sagging Values

Internet pioneer Yahoo! (Nasdaq: YHOO), for example, used to be in the news for blazing new trails in terms of revolutionizing the Internet with its innovations as well as its quirky and flexible culture. That culture included a casual atmosphere charged with enthusiasm, creativity, and innovation. Many of its employees freely and famously worked from home.

Somewhere along the line, though, Yahoo! started to lose its innovative spirit and its competitive culture. The company faltered in the face of its competition. Many observers predicted the company's demise.

Reality Not as It Seems. More recently, though, Yahoo! is in the news for different reasons. In 2012, it brought in a new high-profile CEO, Marissa Mayer, formerly of Google, to turn the stagnant company around. From a numbers point of view, she's done that on the surface. Yahoo!'s stock price initially climbed, and quarterly earnings exceeded expectations. The financial reality, however, isn't quite as it seems. Analysts point to Yahoo!'s earnings as being a result of the company's holdings in Chinese Internet wonder Alibaba, and not as a result of Yahoo's core performance. More recently, however, as Yahoo! sold off part of its Alibaba stake and then that company debuted on the New York Stock Exchange, Yahoo's stock price plummeted.[5][6] By the end of 2014, it had recovered somewhat.[7]

Sagging Morale. Employee morale may be another story, too. In 2013, Mayer suddenly and without warning abolished Yahoo's highly touted work-from-home policy. Employees, long allowed freedom to choose their work locale, suddenly and across the board were banned from working outside of the company's offices. That meant little job flexibility, especially for working parents who depended on it.

At around that same time, CEO Mayer had her first child. To accommodate her new policy, she had a private nursery built for her son next door to her office at Yahoo!. Other parents at Yahoo! don't have that same luxury. They're just out of luck when it comes to spending time with their kids.

Culture Disconnect. What this culture shift from the top down means for Yahoo! long term remains to be seen. Nonetheless, it appears that Mayer isn't concerned about whether her employees and other leaders lead positive professional or personal lives.

It's the bottom dollar right now that counts. The message her actions send to her teams: we don't care about your personal life. Just get the job done.

Better Approach to Sustain Growth

Mayer correctly recognized that changing Yahoo! meant changing the culture. But she took the strategic shortcut. Rather than work with her teams to re-energize the culture and the business to sustain growth long term, she preferred a unilateral shock to "fix" things for immediate results.

Adding to the problem with her strategy and the disconnect from entrenched company values, Mayer doesn't always model the behavior she expects from her employees.

At a recent Qlik customer summit, outspoken entrepreneur billionaire Mark Cuban offered true wisdom on leaders: great leaders don't expect anything of their team or their people that they wouldn't do themselves.

Enabling Strategy

Culture eats strategy for breakfast. Those wise words are most often attributed to Peter Drucker, management consultant, author, and businessman. More to the point, culture—and the values that create it—enables strategy. Together, they make up a company's roadmap to success. Remember culture and its accompanying values lay the foundation for the processes, procedures, and strategies that companies lay out to accomplish specific goals.

Time will tell whether Mayer's choice of strategy works. But, repeatedly other companies have found that if they and their leaders lay the right foundation (focus) via culture, model the right behavior—as in values, give their employees freedom and flexibility, and hold them accountable for results, a workforce will give 150 percent.

Big Disconnect

Essential to success in the above equation is focus. The way we work matters. I know from experience, and studies also show, that the majority of people can work harder, and not as a result of dictatorial bosses who take away privileges and demand immediate results.

Misaligned Actions

Too often, people work on things that don't align with the accomplishing of a company's real goals. Leaders specifically set those goals as part of overarching strategies aimed at creating a smoothly operating system.

The disconnect may be prompted by processes and procedures that are too cumbersome, or values that are too confusing. Communications may be too clouded, or misguided leaders may simply substitute one goal *they think* more important for another.

Whatever the reasons for the disconnect, real values and goals become lost somewhere in the middle. The end result often derails the company's achievement of its goals within allotted time frames and, in the end, its long-term financial success. Again it's about your company as that system of gears. When one cog is out of sync, the entire system locks up, and the company goes nowhere. No one can afford that disconnect, or for their forward momentum to stall for even a moment.

Wasted Time and Effort

In the average business, most workers don't work on the right things in the right way, according to Tor Dahl, economist, productivity expert, and chairman emeritus of the World Confederation of Productivity Science. He has even quantified the disconnect. No matter how hard someone works, that individual actually can increase productivity by at least 30 percent, he says.[8]

Dahl blames the disconnect on organizational ills that include lack of clear directions and goals, processes that aren't optimized, excessive paperwork and reporting requirements, unproductive meetings, and inappropriate systems and tools.

The Hay Group also identified weaknesses in company performance due to the constant struggle with this goals/strategies disconnect.[9]

Focus on Success

E-tailer Zappos! certainly didn't suffer from the disconnect—just the opposite—with its laser focus on customer service as the driver of its meteoric rise.

That kind of focus differentiated Blue Cross Blue Shield of North Carolina (BCBSNC), too, from its competition in an era when other health insurance providers faced harsh criticism.

BCBSNC, the largest insurer in that state, early on focused on readiness for the changes in our health-care system associated with the *Patient Protection and Affordable Care Act*. The company's CEO, Brad Wilson, also linked those changes with improving health care and making it more affordable. "We came up with the ways to embody the kind of change we needed," he told me recently, "We were going to be collaborative, committed, creative, and caring."

His approach worked, too. For the past two years the company has been recognized as one of the World's Most Ethical Companies by Ethisphere Institute. It adopted fee schedules favorable to its clients (not charging clients copays, for example, with the purchase of most generic prescriptions). It established blogs as outlets for patient discussion and complaints, and it follows up on blog comments, questions, and criticism.[10]

While other insurance companies and states struggled with sign-up under the new health insurance laws, BCBSNC took the lead. It opened retail stores in malls across the state to facilitate sign-up. Through all this, the company's revenues soared—up 60 percent in 2013 from the year before.[11]

My Secret to Total Alignment . . . VSE

How then does the average company avoid the disconnect between actions and goals, and ensure that leaders and employees stick to the plan?

It's simple—VSE. I make it a part of every business initiative. VSE is an acronym that spells out the specific short- and long-range set of accomplishments for the company and its team members:

- Vision: the long-term, overarching outlook/goal for a company; encompasses a company's values; to be the most trusted provider and deliver world-class outcomes to customers, for example; visions should be reviewed annually.
- Strategy: an overarching plan of action that includes goals that need to be accomplished in the short term with an eye to achieving a long-term vision; improve employee skill sets, for example, to facilitate faster response time, boost customer satisfaction; or administer employee engagement survey and listen to and act on input.
- Execution: delivering on the strategies to achieve the vision; for example, increase production by 25 percent, while also keeping employees happy and engaged, customers satisfied, and giving back to the community as deliverables.

Over the years, my teams developed VSE and variations on it to facilitate application of the values and culture of a particular company. It's a roadmap and a yardstick for company operations now and in the future.

Alignment Leads to Success

VSE works because it is a one-page document that clearly spells out the company's values, current vision related to those values, strategy to achieve that vision, and the very specific goals required for success. All leaders create their own VSE for their team that reflects their part of the company's overall VSE. It's their go-to "elevator pitch" that they know backward and forward, and utilize when making decisions at all times. That may sound dictatorial, but it works.

When all hands have quick access to the company's VSE, it's easier to know what's expected, to stay focused, and to make decisions based on the real goals at hand. Leaders then can avoid making decisions that derail goals. The result is enhanced performance on the part of the company, its employees, and its leaders. Everyone focuses on accomplishing the same essential goals, hence no disconnect.

A Measure of Accomplishment

Because a VSE lays out the deliverables associated with specific goals, it is a measuring stick, too, for opportunities and performance reviews. Even the smallest teams need to measure their performance against goals, to identify how they're doing for the year—whether you've followed through on a strategy, for example, and/or achieved a vision. I recommend that at least quarterly, companies make their assessments to find out whether they've accomplished the agreed-upon necessary deliverables to achieve their goals.

If they have not, it could be an indication that goals or strategies need rethinking and/or reworking. Team members might not be equipped with the necessary skills to deliver on a goal, for example. That would necessitate a strategy shift to include training.

While I was at Allscripts, the company planned a new product launch. One of the goals associated with that launch was to make sure everyone on the team had the skills necessary to deliver sales results.

Our strategy to accomplish that included a one-day training session. A half-day was devoted to learning about the product (analytics), and the other half-day was spent teaching people how to understand data and metrics in order to help them make better decisions and provide better feedback to leaders about what needed to be done to accomplish the stated goals.

More Tools

I first was introduced to a version of VSE years ago while at Cisco. The one-page VSE was one of the tools the company used to drive alignment between strategies and goals.

At Allscripts, we also utilized the VSE approach. As part of that, the company sponsored an annual Organizational Alignment Day. The point of the day-long event was, as you would imagine, to make sure everyone understood where the company was going, what was expected, and how the company planned to get there. Every leader throughout the company, with the help of Allscripts' Intranet, had a page dedicated to the organizational alignment of his or her department or division. The page included a video highlighting the goals leaders set for the year.

On that particular day, the company also launched a competition, with the winner as the team or division that first achieved its goals during the year. The prize was international company recognition (at no cost to the company!) along with some small monetary reward (in some instances, a gift certificate to a local restaurant).

These successful approaches to alignment, direction, and control (along with positive reinforcement) can serve as a framework that most any company can implement on a smaller scale.

The bottom line is that you and your company have a choice to be intentional and committed to developing a deep values-based culture that creates an inherent way of life and action, or not. The former should be your choice for long-term success.

Staying Value of Culture

Basic values are just that. They are entrenched in and are a part of your life.

John Morgridge, chairman emeritus of Cisco, was a leader in establishing the company's strong giveback culture. He led the company in its early years, joining it as president and CEO in 1988 and growing revenues from just over $5 million to more than $1 billion. Today he remains a staunch supporter of education, conservation, and human services initiatives.

Morgridge also was known at Cisco for his frugality and insistence on a culture to match. In those early years, Morgridge required staff to fly only coach class, no matter how long or how far an airplane flight. When people complained that they weren't upgraded to first class on long flights,

Morgridge at a company meeting showed a slide of himself seated in a plane's coach class putting on an eye mask and complimentary socks with a blanket around his shoulders. The caption read, "Virtual First Class." That's one of those moments you remember forever.

Another of his early admonitions: if you walked out the door of your hotel and couldn't see your car's headlights, your hotel was too expensive.

Morgridge, now a billionaire, recently held what he pegged as his "last company meeting" in Palo Alto, California. Basically it was a reunion of many of the original cast from Cisco's meteoric rise—myself included. Picture a room full of 200 people, many of them some of the most successful business leaders today. It was an ideal setting for a classically elegant meal. Morgridge ordered Domino's pizza for everyone.

Culture Check/Your Company's Values

Now it's your turn to assess your own company's culture with the help of a Culture Audit. For the best results, the audit should be company wide. That includes you, your team members, leaders, and bosses. If everyone is honest in their answers, the results should paint a clear picture of where your company is on the road to developing a positive values-based culture.

Even if you already have what you think is a strong values-based culture, the audit can flag weaknesses and potential flaws before they become serious problems.

If you opt to do a Culture Audit individually, you'll end up with a snapshot of the company you work for and its current values. If those values don't match your own, that could signal it's time for you to look at work opportunities elsewhere.

Start by rating the company and its leadership in terms of some of the essential values listed below. You may want to use a formal rating system— perhaps on a scale of 1 to 5, with 5 the highest or best rating. With each value and answer, get the details—the why or why not, what's right and what isn't.

- *Credibility: Do you trust your company, managers, and leaders? Do the company, its management, and its leadership follow through and do what's promised for team members, customers, and the community? Or do they promise one thing and do another?*

- *Respect: Do you feel like the company respects you as an employee? Do the company's actions reflect respect? Does the company treat and communicate with its employees and customers openly and honestly?*
- *Fairness: Does the company treat all its employees and customers fairly? Are discipline, perks, and details handed out arbitrarily? Do leaders practice unabashed favoritism?*
  - *Be careful how you respond to the questions about your company's fairness to employees and customers. You may not know all the details of a situation, and therefore not understand fully the problem. If someone thinks the company is unfair, find out why. A disgruntled employee may think the company unfair if he or she was passed over for a promotion because of his or her skill levels. That could signal something very different happening, as opposed to if several employees feel a manager treats them unfairly.*
- *Pride: Are you proud to work for the company? Do you take pride in the work you do? What about your company's product or service?* Engaged and happy employees take pride in their company and all that they and the company do. Remember, employee engagement is an essential ingredient in creating a long-term successful company.
- *Camaraderie: Do employees work together, collaborate, and communicate as a team with specific goals in mind? Or is yours a company of lots of lone wolves, each with his or her own agenda?* Think about the importance of everyone's working toward the same goals as a team. That's a key ingredient in long-term success.
- *And is it fun? Do you enjoy going to work every day?* That can be the reality if your company promotes a strong, values-based culture.

Now decide what specific values matter to you, your company, and your community—your customers. It should be a companywide discussion that starts from the top because culture comes from the top. Also keep in mind that corporate culture and values are not a function of the Human Resources Department. Too often, people figure an HR directive or something else as insignificant creates culture. Instead, your company's leaders own the culture, with HR as an enabling organization.

Ask the following questions:

- *What are the values that matter to you?*
- *What values matter to your company?*
- *What values matter to the community and your customers?*

True culture is pervasive. Think about your immediate environment, and how and what you can influence.

Ask more questions:

Are you living the stated values of the company? If the company doesn't have stated values, can you create a set of high values within your own team? That could be a good starting point to show others in the company how and why values do matter.

For example, if your company is a restaurant, an easy way to support the value Social Responsibility/Giveback would be to look at ways in which to donate your product to the community.

You must set up goals for your company, too.

Does your company have goals and strategies associated with those goals? Goals alone mean little without strategies to reach those goals. Goals are important too because they are the implementation of a company's values that reflect the company's culture.

As I mentioned earlier, at Qlik a value is Moving Fast, with the strategy of Discover, Decide, Do. In other words, before you make the move quickly, pause to think and collaborate, and then move to get the desired result.

PART II

Creating the WOW Factor

CHAPTER 3

The Little Things Make a Big Difference

Excellence begins by focusing on the little things that matter.
—*Diane K. Adams*

Building a great culture starts with recognizing the values that are important, and then building them into all aspects of a company. Successful companies, their employees, and customers, though, will tell you, it's the little things that make the big difference when it comes to culture and perpetuating a company's long-term financial success.

Conversely, companies shouldn't consider that those little things alone are enough, without the strong values and competitive wages that go along with it.

The Value of Caring

People don't care what you know until they know you care. Employees join and stay with companies when they feel valued, are challenged, learn, and contribute.

Companies must invest in their employees. That investment doesn't have to always be financial, but it does need to be personal.

The same is true with your customers. They, too, must feel valued and know you care. In today's competitive business world, people expect the basics like good products and/or services. But it's the little things that will differentiate you from your competition.

Let's look at a few examples that do (and don't) make the difference for both employees and customers.

Personal Pizzazz

Before I joined Allscripts, then-CEO Glen Tullman by chance found out I loved chocolate chip cookies, so he promptly sent me a box of to-die-for cookies. I knew he was trying to woo me to join the company. Yet, for a CEO of a major company with thousands of employees to stop and take the time to do something that personal, left an indelible impression on me. So much so, that I began to think about what it might be like to work for someone who cared that much, and who paid such attention to the little things.

A month later, I still hadn't decided whether to join Allscripts, and Tullman sent another box of the cookies.

Those personal touches—I call them WOWs—didn't stop when I eventually joined Allscripts. Glen later found out that ice cream trumped chocolate chip cookies in my book, so you guessed it: he had my favorite ice cream delivered to our house.

It turned out, too, that his personal concern for others wasn't a manufactured ploy to get me or anyone else to join his team. It was a genuine value that was a crucial aspect of the Allscripts' culture Glen worked hard to instill in his company and its teams.

His caring extended to customers. A major player in the electronic medical records world, members of the Allscripts' team frequently had the opportunity to participate in various White House forums. We always made it a point to take customers with us to these conferences because we knew it meant a great deal to them.

The Ultimate WOW

One of my favorite WOWs, though, happened while I was with another company. One of my favorite people, Diane Rupert—the recipient of the WOW—still talks about it almost 20 years later.

My team had been working under a lot of stress for months in preparation for a product launch. One morning this particular employee came to work bubbling with excitement. She had just bought a new convertible and was thrilled.

Without hesitation, I told her, "Take the afternoon off and enjoy your new car." It was a simple gesture. New product launch or not, we certainly could do without one team member for one afternoon. Little did I realize at the time that a small gesture could leave such a big and lasting impression. That's one big WOW!

Paying Dividends

To give an employee a few extra hours off didn't take much effort and didn't really cost the company anything additional. The personal gesture, though, paid multiple dividends.

It helped nurture a loyal employee. It bolstered that employee's morale as well as those around her because people understood that we treated employees as the assets they were. And it showed that the company and its leaders were human.

Too often, all that gets lost—along with long-term success—amid today's immediate profits-centric culture.

More Over-the-Top Ideas

More recently Glen and another Allscripts veteran, Lee Shapiro, both now venture capitalists, have been involved in the start-up of another company, Livongo, a consumer digital health company. With the mantra "It's the little things that matter," the company gave each of its team members—at the time 35 employees and growing—the opportunity to send company marketing items to ten friends or family members. Those items ranged from T-shirts to water bottles to a very cool phone amplifier.

The strategy behind the move was to encourage employees to feel great about their product and what they're doing. At the same time, the approach broadens the company's name and brand. Glen and Lee truly know the power of engaged team members.

Small and Big at Same Time

Your company can gain big advantages with simple gestures, too. It starts with believing in and caring about your employees and customers, and taking the time and making the effort for the small gestures that resonate strong values and a culture to match.

My Ice Cream Cure-All

Last summer, after one particularly grueling day of meetings with Qlik executives, I finally made it back to my hotel room around 9 p.m. Exhausted, I had just collapsed on the couch when there was a knock on the door. It was room service with two gigantic bowls of my favorite ice cream—chocolate and butter pecan—courtesy of Qlik's CFO, Tim MacCarick, and general counsel, Debbie Lofton.

It was a small gesture, yet a big personal acknowledgment of the work I had done that day. When people know they're appreciated and their work matters, they're more willing to make the extra effort.

Small Gesture/Big Impact

That kind of personal caring is a value that runs deep at Qlik. Not long ago I had another one of those days at the office that makes you wonder why you're there to begin with. Then, my CEO popped his head in the door and asked if I wanted to grab some Mexican food for lunch.

We were extremely busy and on a deadline, but Lars recognized that going out to lunch would ease tensions and be a good break. It was a simple gesture, yet again instantly conveyed to me that he cared about me and that he and the company valued my contributions.

If you and your team are working hard, consider taking a break. Even treating your colleagues to sodas in the break room can have a positive effect on dislodging differences and roadblocks.

Family Matters

If you've ever been to an out-of-town conference or a business-related event, you know that the CEOs generally get the impressive accommodations stocked with the high-end amenities.

I'm acquainted with one CEO who, whenever he attends a big conference, gives away his accommodations to an employee who has done a great job, or even to a customer. At a recent conference at a mega-resort in Orlando, he gave his palatial digs to a customer whose family had tagged along. It wasn't his company's biggest or best customer. But the CEO figured the kids would enjoy the fancy accommodations, and they did. They had a blast, and the customer never forgot that.

The bottom line: when possible, do something nice not just for an individual but for his or her family, too. They'll remember it, and recognize that you do more than simply talk about positive values. You live them. Doing so is one more part of how to build strong relationships with employees and with customers.

It's those relationships that sustain companies through good and bad economic times.

A Paper Solution to Emulate

At Qlik, we've come up with a great, simple way to recognize the little (or big) things our people do, no matter where they are in the world. It's called Qlik Notes. These are ordinary 3x5 cards with a particular laudable Qlik value preprinted on one side—"Moving Fast" or "Open and Straightforward," for example. The other side of the card is blank.

Atta Boy Note. If an employee or a leader does a great job on something that strongly reflects a particular company value—"Moving Fast," for example—and the employee reacts quickly and appropriately to a lead with the right collaboration and thought behind his or her action, that employee's boss will likely send a Qlik Note. "Moving Fast" would be the value on the front, and the handwritten note on the flip side might read "way to go" or "nice job." It's not a dissertation. It's a simple and quick note that recognizes the employee has done a great job. That little extra makes a big difference.

Your Version. Of course, you and your company don't have to have the preprinted cards, but you do have to care. A hand-scribbled note goes a long way toward building those all-important relationships.

The Quicken Version. At mortgage-lending giant Quicken Loans, CEO Bill Emerson takes the time to personally sign birthday cards to every employee—more than 10,000 of them. Even employees' kids get cards, AND gifts, too.

In case you think little things like that don't matter, Quicken Loans has made the top 30 on CNN/Fortune's 100 Best Places to Work For the last 11 years (It's No. 5 in 2014). Plus, it's grown to the nation's second-largest overall lender with a record $80 billion in home loan volume in 2013.[1]

An Engaged Culture Makes the Difference

Too often, companies and their leaders talk about career development paths and structures. A better approach to long-term business success starts with knowing your people and their interests, and how those interests might dovetail with your company, and then executing with that in mind.

With this approach, your employees are more likely to end up with successful ownership of outcomes—accountability—and hopefully steer the company toward long-term success. All that is a part of creating a culture that engages your employees.

Caring Counts

Your people want and need to know that you give a darn. Companies do that by paying competitive wages, along with engaging and caring about their employees personally and professionally. That means living your company's stated values with your employees as well as customers.

Energizing Performance. Employee engagement is your powerful tool for energizing teams, boosting performance, and bolstering bottom lines. It's essential to a company's long-term success, too.

For those who are skeptical or think engagement is another of those wild, unrealistic concepts that aren't important at "real" businesses, consider some of the numbers from a recent Gallup study.

Numbers Back It Up. Among other things, the study compared the performance of teams with highly engaged employees with those with low employee engagement. The highly engaged teams had 22 percent higher profitability than those with low engagement levels. Those winning teams also had

21 percent greater productivity;

65 percent lower turnover; and

10 percent higher customer ratings.[2]

ENGAGEMENT MATTERS

High-performance managers create an engaging work environment that promotes peak performance in three primary ways. A recent Gallup study, found the following:

High-performance managers are involved in their employees' work lives. They don't subscribe to a laissez-faire approach to management, and they don't ignore their employees. When employees strongly agree that their manager knows what projects or tasks they are working on, they are almost seven times more likely to be engaged than actively disengaged.

High-performance managers help employees set goals and prioritize their projects. Employees who work for a manager who helps them set performance goals are 17 times more likely to be engaged than disengaged.

> *High-performance managers hold their employees accountable for performance. It is not enough to be involved and provide direction. Great managers also ask their employees to take ownership of their success or failure. When managers don't hold employees accountable for performance, about seven in ten employees (69%) are actively disengaged, while only 3 percent are engaged.*
>
> Source: Gallup[3]

The Sky Is the Limit

When teams are engaged, they're motivated and inspired to accomplish great things. They bring the organization's culture and its goals to life.

For example, no matter your political leanings, the 2008 McCain-Obama presidential election is a prime example of the power of engagement. Democratic presidential candidate Barack Obama won the election over Republican John McCain, with both political and other experts clearly pointing to the Obama campaign's communication skills as a differentiator. Despite the odds and the doubters at the time, his team got the word out.

Engage and Inspire. The Obama campaign is a great example of a winning engage-and-inspire-your-troops model. The campaign utilized on-the-ground teams in every possible venue to get his message out. They tapped into the communications and follow-up power available with the latest technologies, especially social media, and his staff utilized his personal interactions to rally support for him.

In a Business Setting. A corporate/business setting is no different, even when applied on a smaller scale. To engage and invest in your team requires a reach that extends to all locations. That means

- making sure everyone gets the message;
- capitalizing on technology—including making sure your team is trained to use *your* technology; and
- employing personal interaction, including commitment and face-to-face contact from the top, to ensure success.

New Approach. A business and its teams can't be afraid to try new, different, and better approaches to getting the word out, either.

Obama's campaign created culture around the use of social media and debuted the late-night talk show circuit as a means of getting the message out. Before the 2008 election, political candidates considered it groveling to visit late-night television shows. Now it's become standard operating procedure for political figures.

Engagement Master

Yet again, I bring up Cisco's John Chambers and his teams as positive examples that reflect what's right with culture. This time, I discuss John as a master at engaging others.

Consistently he makes a point of interacting on a personal level with those people around him. Whether it's an employee, leader, peer, customer, or anyone else, he always takes the time to interact with questions like, "How are you?" and "How is the family?"

Funny thing, too, is that everyone knows he's going to ask those questions. But you still feel like he genuinely cares. It's not just schmoozing; rather, it's making a connection and caring about the person you're talking to or working with.

People in all types and sizes of companies today are driven to make money. But, as John's actions reflect, stopping to establish a relationship and a connection engages that person and organization, and is what makes a business successful long term. That's engagement on steroids.

The Power of Recognition

Don't overlook the power of recognizing and expressing public appreciation of your teams either. Employee recognition programs are the top approach to bolstering employee engagement at best-in-class organizations, according to The Aberdeen Group's 2013 study, "The Power of Employee Recognition."

Aberdeen defines engagement as including organizational priorities as well as employee satisfaction. The effects of recognition are broad and long lasting, their research shows. "By acknowledging an employee's positive behaviors and demonstrating appreciation for employee contributions, that individual worker will continue those behaviors, stay engaged with the company, and feel motivated to perform."[4]

Technology and Other Trump Cards

Don't bother with the argument that you and your company haven't the time or the money to engage others by sending birthday cards, giving employees extra time off, taking trips to big conferences, or handing out cookies and ice cream or good news.

No Excuses

Thanks to technology, there's no excuse today not to pay attention to the little things.

Start with the WOWs. They're simple and easy with the help of smartphones, personal computers (PCs), the Internet, and Intranets. Instant messaging, email, and apps like Skype, FaceTime, WebEx (videoconferencing), and more offer endless possibilities for personalizing interactions and going the extra mile.

Personal conversations about performance, recognition for personal and professional accomplishments, and even simple thank-you notes are a little more than a click away.

And they are the game-changers in developing and cementing relationships and loyalty with employees and with customers.

Combine that with a company culture that values caring and other people, and you have a winning combination for success.

Smile

Believe it or not, your face—even if it's not smiling—and your words of praise make a big difference. When an employee does something special or wins an award, or his or her family member accomplishes something special, it takes only a few minutes for that personal recognition. Pick up a smartphone, or Skype or FaceTime that person and let him or her know you care.

When it's a client's birthday, send an e-card—many are free—or gather the team for a photo holding up a "CONGRATS" card, and then send it as a text message or email.

We all have cell phones and they're great cameras. Use them to your advantage.

You'll notice a difference in the way people—employees as well as customers and the community—perceive you and/or your company. They will see you care.

Personalization with Benefits

One midlevel team leader at a California tech company took caring to a new level with the help of technology. In her competitive market, worker turnover was high.

This leader knew she had to step up her game to cement relationships with distant team members. Consistently and unfailingly, she paid attention to and recognized her team's professional and personal accomplishments—from birthdays to anniversaries, the achievement of professional goals, and more.

My favorite example of her connective prowess is that with the help of a basic web-teleconferencing tool, she held a virtual baby shower for an employee in Singapore. Of course, it was a big hit with everyone. It helped boost morale and build company loyalty, too.

The team leader ended up with the highest employee engagement/satisfaction rate in the more-than-50,000-employee company. That translates into cash at the bottom line when you consider the cost of replacing an employee is 100 to 300 percent of the employee's base salary, according to estimates from the Society of Human Resource Management.[5]

The E-catch

To help reinforce a culture of caring, e-communications are great for the occasional reminder or kudos. But be careful how you use them. An email or a text is NOT an adequate substitute for personal, face-to-face discussions that serious issues require.

Too many leaders fall victim to the e-only craze, with negative repercussions. Consider a few best (and worst) practices.

Epic Failure

No exceptions. Don't criticize or embarrass anyone via email. You'll regret it later.

Don't fire off an email when you're mad, either. Don't even write the email thinking you'll send it later. You'll regret it later, instead.

Over the years I've encountered many an email faux pas. I'm sure most of you, too, have been on either end of email nightmares.

The following are a few instances in which pushing the button on an email undermined what had been a positive and productive culture. In each case, the unfortunate repercussions could have easily been avoided. Your team members need to know these types of e-moves are not tolerated.

Design Failure. A company's design team leader had for weeks been trying to get consensus among his team. On this particular day he was especially frustrated with one individual who had been belligerent and uncooperative in design discussions.

Rather than pick up the phone or opt for face-to-face constructive discussions with that individual, the angry leader fired off a nasty email to him. Inadvertently, he also copied the message to all 12 team members. (Don't gasp too loud. This kind of thing happens all the time.)

That accidental goof crippled the team's once-strong collaborative efficacy. Team members stopped being open and honest in their analysis of designs under discussion. Creativity suffered, and in the end, the team had to be disbanded.

Flame Out. Flame-o-grams are another big email faux pas that employees forward to me all the time, and that can undermine even the best culture. In this case, a leader sends a nasty email to a worker. Usually, the tone of the email implies some variation on "How could you be so stupid?"

That's a big NO. This kind of criticism only torpedoes an organization's effectiveness.

More E-misses

If you decide to set up e-templates—a basic thank-you note, for example—or if you send out blast notes—multiples of the same note—to different people, remember to change the names in the form.

It sounds so small, but so often they're not changed, and that means a big miss in the "personalized" note department. It actually may be worse than no note at all, so beware and be careful.

Criticize in Private

Personal criticism is a private matter not for public consumption. This is very different from in a meeting having open, honest discussions about how to handle a situation.

It's not even OK to openly criticize someone for the purpose of teaching everyone else. There's a better way to learn than throwing someone under the bus as the scapegoat for training purposes. Instead, the approach should be talk about the situation and solutions without pointing fingers.

Beyond the Techno Faults

Not every goof, though, can be blamed on technology. Plenty are simply the result of careless preparation. Goofs are often inadvertent and almost always lead to bad outcomes.

Someone Left Out

A great way to recognize the hard work of an individual or a group is to mention the person or persons and their accomplishments in front of their peers—at all-hands meetings, for example. It's an especially effective method of praise.

The big goof comes when the CEO or leader celebrates a team effort and shares the names of only some of the players, inadvertently leaving someone out. Another slip-up can happen when all the correct individuals are honored on stage, but one or two names might be left out on a document (online or otherwise) that also praises the team.

The moral of these stories is, it's the little details that make the difference.

When the Caring Stops...So Does the Cash Coming In

Just as difficult and impactful as leaving someone out when it comes to praise, is suddenly switching gears and not caring at all.

One company that I've dealt with for years used to be a leader in paying attention to the little things. It also used to be a winning team in terms of financials.

Then recession came. As the company struggled, its top leadership began to focus on the profits-first-and-only mode, dropping many of the caring elements that had created a positive workplace. Reverting to an operational approach, the leaders cut costs across the board to get the bottom line right. That meant taking out all the meaningful little things. Some things that were taken away included free soda and water, as well as energy bars for employees, tokens of appreciation for employees like small-denomination gift cards awarded for a job well done, and more. Community giveback and volunteering in the community was no longer a priority either.

As the company stripped away the little things that make a difference, it lost its strong values-based culture and the hearts of its employees. Working at the company today has become a job to be tolerated. It's no longer a great place for someone to work and learn and grow.

To its leaders' surprise, the company's "new and improved" approach had the opposite financial effect. Even with big layoffs, financial performance is off. Attrition is up, too, which means more expenses to replace those people, because the reason people stay—the company's high values—is gone.

Long-term success at the bottom line demands leaders who lead with not only their heads but also their hearts. They must care about their employees and their customers. They have to pay attention to the little things if they hope to sustain success over the long haul.

"Little Things" Success Story I

At the other end of the success spectrum, consider the case of High Point University. Its president, Nido R. Qubein, believes in the importance of those little things and, applied on a grand scale, this perspective has made a world of difference.

Big Changes

High Point used to be a small school with about 1,000 students in rural High Point, North Carolina. The school watched and struggled as education costs spiraled out of control. That was a decade and more than $225 million in donations ago before Nido took the university's helm and consciously decided to up its game.[6]

A tough businessman and successful motivational speaker, he knew the university faced stiff competition and that it desperately needed to grow. He also understood that culture could be the differentiator and ignite sustained growth. So he made the conscious effort and changes necessary to position High Point as a university with a strong, individual-based, caring culture.

Nido created that culture from the top down with lots of intentional little actions that added up and fostered success. Enrollment skyrocketed.

Among some of those little things are the following:

Consciously using positive, clear language to encourage extraordinary actions. The entry to the campus, for example, is on a street named

"Extraordinary Way." The goal is to encourage students and faculty to strive to achieve their own individual excellence.

Embracing diversity. High Point consciously embraces all kinds of diversity—ethnic, religious, cultural, and more. Students and faculty are welcomed for their individuality, not their conformity. The university's most recent freshman class included students from 17 foreign countries and 44 states, plus the District of Columbia.

Opening an on-campus steakhouse, in part to teach etiquette. Students are required to eat there monthly to help them learn the appropriate etiquette at a business meal.

Establishing kiosks across campus to dispense free yogurt, water, and granola. The concept is that students are important and are not just numbers.

Installing computerized monitors across campus that advertise the milestones of individual students. If it's your birthday, for example, the monitors broadcast the news to everyone.

Forget the Naysayers

As expected, Nido and High Point have their critics. The naysayers point to the little things as trivial and Nido as an opportunist. They claim he's turned High Point into nothing more than a party school.

But the numbers tell the real story, and put the naysayers in perspective.

Education Leader Today

With the changes at High Point, financial donations to the university soared and so did construction projects. Today, High Point is one of the top regional private colleges in the South with two campuses—one in High Point and another in Winston-Salem. Enrollment has more than quadrupled, to approximately 4,200 undergraduate and graduate students from more than 46 states and 27 countries.

The university has been ranked No. 1 as the top Regional College (South) by *U.S. News and World Report* since 2013.[7] The university's success has impacted its community, too. Statewide its economic impact is in excess of $370 million per year.[8]

That's bottom-line success. So much for the culture critics and naysayers.

"Little Things" Success Story II

Paying attention to the little things works on a smaller scale, too, and in difficult as well as good economic times.

Strata Decision Technology is a Chicago-based small business with about 100 employees. The formerly family-owned company, which develops financial and analytical software for the health-care field, was searching to find its financial way when it was bought out by Veronis Suhler Stevenson, a private global investment firm, in 2011.

Eye on Growth

The new owners, like High Point's Qubein, knew that to grow long term and achieve its potential, the company needed strong leadership and a values-based culture with set expectations to follow.

Strata Decisions brought in a seasoned veteran (and culture expert), Dan Michelson, to lead the company. Dan is the former chief marketing and strategy officer for Allscripts (we worked together there), at which, in his 12 years with that organization, he helped grow it from 100 employees to more than 7,000, and from $26 million in annual revenues to more than $1.4 billion.[9]

Intentional Effort

Dan knows the importance of building the right culture and paying attention to the small details. Our success, he told me, is the result of doing a lot of those little things that add up. Among some of the "little things" he did at Strata Decisions that motivate, energize, and make a difference for employees are

- providing free beverages and water for employees (which sounds minor, but which is a major morale booster);
- recognizing outstanding achievements, including setting up a Wall of Fame at the company's headquarters;
- changing the compensation policy from monthly to weekly paychecks (because employees told him that it was tough to budget one paycheck over a month's time);
- requiring every employee to anonymously rate his performance as CEO, with the results presented to his board of directors. That's accountability.

Upbeat Culture

If attrition and the bottom line are any indicator, Dan's belief that the little things add up is spot on. The once-struggling company was named to *Inc. Magazine*'s list of the 5,000 fastest growing private companies in 2013 and 2014.[10] Dan says attrition at the company—and the costs associated with it—dropped, too, from 33 percent after the takeover to just 12 percent at the end of 2013.

In talking to the employees, it is possible to see that the strategy clicks, too.

Walk into the company, and everyone's smiling, even those people sitting at their desks. They're not the mannequin-like people you might see in a sci-fi thriller in which everyone walks around with a wired Willy Wonka smile. These are employees who are upbeat about their jobs and their lives; they're enthusiastic, friendly, and genuine, and enjoy talking about their company and its achievements, and how they give back to the community. A huge wallboard announces personal achievements of the staff. Posted sign-up sheets advertise for community volunteers to help with various causes.

This is a company, the leaders of which know how to create an extraordinary environment for achievement and excellence.

Culture Check/The Little Things

People—whether employees, customers, or the community—don't care what you know until they know how much you care. That's worth repeating.

How do you, your company, and its leaders rate when it comes to valuing and caring about employees, customers, and the community? Ask the following questions of your leadership, or, if your leaders won't take the time to answer, ask yourself. (Hint: if your leaders are "too busy," then maybe those "little things" aren't a priority at your company.)

Let's assume your company is rolling out a new product tomorrow. How would your leader/leaders respond to the following scenarios?

A team member's 10-year-old son falls ill at school, and the team member asks whether it's OK to leave for the rest of the day. How would you or your leadership respond?

"That's too bad. We have work to do."

"You can run home during your lunch hour, but then come back. There's just too much to do before tomorrow's rollout."

"No problem. We can manage without you. Family comes first."

A team member's aunt, with whom she's very close, is diagnosed with a brain tumor. The octogenarian lives by herself and is several hundred miles away. Your team member wants to be with her aunt. How would you or your leadership respond?

"Great. If you miss work, we'll have to replace you."

"No problem. You can take a leave of absence—without pay, of course. You'll have a job when you come back, but it will be whatever is available."

"We understand the importance of family and will work with you on whatever it takes to make your job work."

A customer calls on the phone to complain that your company's product doesn't solve his problem. How would your leadership respond?

"You bought it, you're stuck with it."

"We know it's not the right product for the customer's needs, but don't tell him that. Convince him that he's not using it right."

"Let's talk further about this. We really thought our product could solve your issues. But perhaps we were wrong. If so, of course we'll take the product back and help you find something that works better."

With each situation, the final scenario is the best and is the standard way of operating at companies with positive, values-based cultures. If that's not what happens at your company, then it's time to make changes or to make a change in your job.

CHAPTER 4

R-E-S-P-E-C-T: It Goes with Integrity

Respect is the greatest gift you can give another.

—*Diane K. Adams*

Plenty of companies and their leaders talk about integrity and respect in the workplace. Yet just as with many of the other positive values, only the very best actually practice it.

The disconnect can be conscious or subconscious, but the results are the same. Lack of integrity and respect for your employees, and in turn your customers, translates directly to the bottom line.

Respect and integrity is about honesty in what's said and done, workplace diversity, and inclusion. It's also about building a culture that truly values people for the differences they bring to the table, whether race, gender, lifestyle, way of thinking, or something else. And it's about treating people with dignity and decency when they join your company as well as when they leave.

Beware the Message—Especially with Firing

Bob had worked at his company for seven years. He was a great guy. Everyone liked him. But the company felt his job performance wasn't up to par and decided to release him.

Part of Doing Business

As unfortunate as it is to lay someone off, tough staffing decisions—including layoffs—are an integral part of doing business. No company can afford to foot the bill for employees who don't carry their weight, or to pay huge salaries for routine work simply because that person has been in the same job so long. That happens all the time with companies that don't pay attention to strategic staffing issues.

Unacceptable Approach

In Bob's case, the problem wasn't that his company had to let him go. It was how the company went about firing this long-time loyal and honest employee. The company didn't take the typical approach of first trying to work with the employee—in this instance, Bob—to help him improve, or even establishing a record of his poor performance that included warnings, follow-up memos, and so on as protection against any legal repercussions of his ouster.

Instead, one day Bob's manager called him into her office and told him, "You're fired. The security guard outside will escort you to the door. We'll send you your things."

That was it. No warnings, no respect, no dignity, no integrity, and no explanation. This sounds unbelievable in today's workplace, in which companies usually worry about repercussions that can accompany employee firings. But rules, regulations, and fear of lawsuits or not, this kind of disrespect is a very real problem that happens all too often.

At this writing, it's the beginning of 2015, and already a similarly dismissed and disgraced employee of another company has complained to me about the same scenario. She told me her boss called her into the office on the pretense of a sales meeting, told her she was fired, took away her computer, and told her to leave the office immediately. The employee said she was given no warning, no explanation, and no opportunity even to contact her clients about pending deals.

That kind of dismissal isn't acceptable. Most any individual—barring those who have flagrantly violated stated codes of conduct—should have the opportunity to leave with dignity.

Pay attention to firing. How you fire someone—whether a single person or tens of thousands of people at once—is as important as how you hire them. That's because of the message this action conveys at a time when everyone is watching.

Successful companies respect their employees and always treat them with integrity. Without provocation, Bob's company kicked him to the curb. He wasn't allowed to go back to his office, sign off his computer, clean out his desk, or even say goodbye to any of his colleagues of the last seven years. That was how this company treated a loyal employee!

Clear, negative message. Worse still, those kinds of actions send a clear message to the company's other employees and to its customers and the community: "We don't care about you or anyone else." At the bottom line, these kinds of actions torpedo morale because no one wants to go the extra mile for, or be associated with a company (and its products or services) that doesn't care.

A Better Way

At one point Cisco determined that layoffs were prudent and necessary to survive changes in the industry and the economy. The idea of layoffs was especially tough because of the company's strong culture that emphasized teamwork, collaboration, and social responsibility.

Positive spin. The Culture and Talent team there came up with a unique and positive spin on what could have been a much less palatable situation. The company provided a generous severance package that included cash as well as job-placement assistance. The best aspect of the package was that all 2,000 employees to be laid off were given an additional option. Instead of taking the severance package, they could work one year at a nonprofit organization of their choice and receive 50 percent of their salary—plus the severance bonuses, insurance coverage, and so on—while doing so.

Kudos for Meaningfulness. That's one of the most creative, values-based approaches to layoffs that I've ever seen. The company treated its departing employees with dignity, integrity, and respect, while maintaining alignment with its core values. What a great way to give departing employees a paid and important purpose while they look for a new job.

How You Can Lay Off Employees with Dignity

Not every company is as big as Cisco or can afford large severance packages, or to carry an employee at half-salary for one year. But you can and must treat your departing employees—whether one, 100, 1,000, or more—with respect, honesty, integrity, and above all, dignity.

I've had to lay off individuals many times at different companies. Unless there's a specific reason not to trust someone—the hot-tempered leader whom I let go in the last chapter is a good example—escorting them out the door á la Bob's experience is NOT how to do it.

Saving face and with grace. In Bob's case, he had been a loyal employee. A better approach to releasing him would have been to give him either 24 hours to leave or the option to let his team know he was leaving and then stay another week. That would have allowed Bob to save face and leave in a respectful manner. And that would have conveyed the message to others that the company cares and values its employees.

Clarify responsibilities. In a case like Bob's, however, leadership must be very clear on the departing employee's responsibilities.

For example, he or she should understand it's not acceptable to bad-mouth the company. One way to ensure that happens is to link the employee's compliance with that responsibility to his or her receipt of a portion of the severance package. That motivates the departing employee to keep his or her comments to him- or herself before and after he or she has left.

The bottom line is that when someone must exit your company, the situation should be handled with respect and aligned with the positive values that are the foundation for your company's culture.

This approach limits negative internal and external backlash.

The Importance of Caring. In case you think the idea of backlash is an overreaction, consider how you would feel if you were an honest and loyal employee, and your employer unceremoniously told you to get out. I'm sure you wouldn't think too kindly of that employer. And how would your fellow employees feel if you were booted out?

I know from experience that they wouldn't harbor much loyalty to the employer or willingness to go the extra mile for a company that had so little respect for individuals, especially for someone who had given so much to the company for so long.

When a company doesn't care, neither do its employees. Customers feel this attitude, too, and it's only a matter of time before performance, product, and balance sheets suffer.

The Gold Standard. Not long ago, Vedder Price, a Chicago-based legal firm, faced a restructuring that resulted in 39 layoffs. The company has more than 300 attorneys, in addition to assistants, and service and administrative employees worldwide.

Firm President and CEO Michael Nemeroff is a strong advocate of a culture based on long-term relationships. So, throughout the layoff process he wanted to make sure the company's culture of respect and integrity continued. How he accomplished that is a model that others can easily emulate:

- The company offered to place the displaced employees at jobs in other locations of the company.
- Every departing employee received a generous severance package that included cash as well as health insurance coverage and job-placement assistance. (Outplacement is important because it lets employees—current and exiting—know that the company cares.)
- In some cases, departing employees' jobs were outsourced. Vedder Price in turn worked with the outsourcers to hire the soon-to-be-laid-off employees.
- The company honored its 39 departing employees with a party to celebrate their contributions to the company. (A note of caution about the idea of a celebration, however: again, be careful of the message you convey at a time when everyone is watching. Not everyone may understand the financial differences between the one-time expense of a party vs. the ongoing expenses of a full-time employee.)

THE MINIMUM SEVERANCE PACKAGE

Departing employees—other than those dismissed because of poor performance—should be given some type of severance to help them transition and start over. In an ideal situation, that package should include:

- minimum salary severance—one to three months depending on years of service;
- outplacement services (the company should make that first outplacement appointment for the exiting employee to give him or her a place to start a new job search); and
- health insurance coverage for a minimum length of the severance.

Autocratic Leadership

At the opposite end of the spectrum from Vedder Price is a workplace that lacks integrity and respect for others. Usually controlled by an autocratic leader, this micromanaging boss governs as a tyrant.

Remember the manufacturing company I talked about in chapter 1 that saw a 20 percent drop in production because of tyrannical leadership? The plant managers' iron-fisted rule didn't discriminate against anyone. The leaders had disdain, distrust, and disrespect for everyone. And the company's production plummeted until the autocratic rulers were removed and their leadership policies changed.

Behavioral Expectations

I worked with one company in which the top leaders insisted that disrespect for others absolutely would not be tolerated. With that in mind, the company's leaders participated in internal 360 feedback assessments that included responses from peers and employees.

Those assessments identified one long-time team leader whose autocratic management style did not reflect the company's values. In fact, members of his team had indicated they planned to leave the company if he didn't change.

It was my job to follow up and debrief the individual about his misguided management style. I was also supposed to work with him to change his approach.

I expected a chilly reception, but his reaction still stuns me. On the Wednesday afternoon before the long Thanksgiving weekend, I walked into his office. Predictably, he wasn't pleased to see me. He tolerated my verbal review of the assessments. But he didn't care what I had to say, and then basically turned me around and sent me out the door.

I spent the holiday weekend girding myself for the expected showdown and blowup that following Monday. But was I surprised by what happened. After four days off work, on Monday the leader called me into his office, closed the door behind me, and said, "I'm ready to listen."

Not only did he listen but he also embraced the feedback as constructive and valuable criticism. He used it as a guide to change how he dealt with others. Instead of being autocratic and dictatorial, he became pragmatic and collaborative. His approach became even-handed, honest, and direct. His team rallied behind him, too. No one quit.

Working Together

It's amazing what can happen when a company's leadership is committed to honesty and integrity, when those leaders are willing to make the tough decisions that go along with that, and when the rest of the company recognizes that commitment, takes it to heart, and embraces it.

That's a strong values-based culture in action from the top down.

Subtle Disrespect

Lack of integrity and respect in the workplace isn't always as blatant as a misguided leader out to dominate everyone in everything that's said and done.

Ignoring Consensus

Lack of integrity and respect can be subtle, too. One of the most common situations is when a leadership team comes together to discuss an issue, irons out differences in opinion, reaches a consensus, and then the boss walks out of the room and proceeds to ignore what was decided.

If you or anyone else makes a commitment, stick to it. Otherwise, it's a breach of your and your company's integrity.

Unilateral Decision-making

Another common integrity breach that has no place in a values-based culture is when decisions—especially people issues—are made without regard to process and guidelines.

Regularly, I see leaders ignoring the vetting process for senior-level promotions in favor of their preferred candidate. There's a reason for a standardized vetting process, especially at leadership levels. The system is there to ensure that a candidate chosen for a job has the skills and support needed for that job.

The White Lies

If you're running late to a meeting or can't make a deliverable, forget the contrived excuses. They don't get you off the hook. Instead, those little white lies show a lack of integrity and respect for others.

The white lies that especially bother me are those that involve someone who is late for a meeting, who says, "I'm on the way," when in reality, his or her last meeting hasn't even ended yet. In other cases, someone doesn't make a deliverable and has a dozen excuses for why he or she missed the deadline.

In both instances, what's wrong with the truth? It's better to be honest and accept the reality and the truth. Your peers and your customers will respect you more for it.

Beyond your honesty and integrity being at stake a missed deliverable—a design team didn't deliver its portion of a product solution, for example—can have a huge impact. It's up to bosses and peers to pay attention to the real reasons behind the delays. Perhaps the team's leader is trying to manage too much, doesn't have the real expertise needed to deliver, or simply messed up and is unwilling to accept the responsibility.

We're All Human

The opposite of autocratic leadership is a leader who recognizes that everyone is human. As part of that, we all can and do make innocent mistakes. Accepting those mistakes reflects the ultimate in respect for others.

No Small Mistakes

No matter how big and far-reaching, an innocent mistake is just that, an innocent mistake. How leaders react to the mistake can reflect their greatness in terms of their honesty and integrity, or their lack thereof in the form of autocratic behavior that seeks to level blame.

Big Faux Pas. While at Cisco, an executive assistant to Rick Justice (the head of sales at the time) made what could have been a career-altering mistake. While editing Rick's remarks for an upcoming earnings call with analysts, she accidentally clicked the wrong icon on her computer screen. Instead of sending the edited comments only to Rick, she sent them to 15,000 people, preannouncing the earnings. It was a move that potentially could have had a dramatic effect on markets and more.

The normally great, always-on-the-mark employee was horrified. She immediately accepted the blame, but that didn't solve the problem because it was no small mistake.

Rather than berate the assistant, both Rick and then-CEO John Chambers chose the path of integrity. John walked up to her and graciously pointed out that no matter how far-reaching, the mistake was an innocent one. "Let's fix it now," he told her, and they did. They immediately called a meeting with analysts and released earnings ahead of schedule.

How great it is to work for a boss and a company that don't berate or level blame, and that work hard to promote honesty, integrity, and respect for others.

My Big Mistake

I've made my share of blunders, too. But as happened at Cisco, I've been lucky enough to work for and with great companies and leaders who understand that we're all human and that mistakes are made.

One of my biggest mistakes involved compensation inequities, the result of my enthusiasm to get the job done without truly assessing the entire situation. I initially favored an increase in pay rates for certain production employees. My boss decided against it. Case over. Well, not exactly.

Not long afterwards, I changed jobs and became head of Human Resources. I still worked for the same boss who had overruled me on pay raises. One day, one of our leaders requested 65 workers with a specific skill. I found all 65 workers already trained in the skill set at a struggling company. I figured, correctly, that it would be more effective and efficient for my employer if we brought in already trained workers.

Without thinking it through, I offered the workers the higher pay rate— the same higher rate my superiors had rejected earlier. The big problem with that decision was that suddenly 65 people were earning more than 1,000 others doing the same job.

As soon as I realized what I had done, I was horrified. In my excitement to find trained new hires, I made an honest, unintentional mistake. I didn't purposely overrule my superiors or act out of spite, and they knew it, because they knew my level of integrity. Unfortunately, though, my mistake cost the company a small fortune because in turn it had to raise the pay rates of all the same-level employees.

I remember my boss graciously told me, "OK, Diane, this happened. But let's move on." He didn't lecture me. No one knew better than I what my mistake had cost the company.

All-Inclusive Workplace Essential

Integrity and respect also translate into an all-inclusive workplace. Successful companies embrace diversity and the differences each person offers in terms of talent and experiences, as well as race, religion, gender, and more.

It's in this spirit of collaborative and creative differences that these companies achieve excellence.

The Ultimate in Sexism

One of the shining stars in a technology company was a young woman with incredible potential. She always won the company's top awards for sales and marketing, excelled in creativity, and was a master at communication and collaboration.

Then she and her husband had a child. The first day the new mom returned to work after six weeks of pregnancy leave, she walked into the office, enthusiastic and excited. She'd just finished greeting her colleagues when her manager called her into his office and demanded to know how she intended to deliver strong results now that work no longer was her top priority.

This wasn't in the 1960s or '80s, or even in the '90s. This actually happened not long ago in what was supposed to be a progressive workplace with enlightened leaders.

Horrified by her boss' blunt prejudices, the once-highly touted software engineer ended up leaving the company. Despite the fact that the boss' behavior likely was a blatant violation of workplace antidiscrimination policy, this young woman simply was unwilling to work in that kind of environment.

Respect and Work/Life Balance

Successful companies also know the importance of work/life balance for helping employees work at their potential. They understand that the definition of family today isn't as typical as it once might have been. Parents—whether single or in a couple—have child-care responsibilities and child needs.

Flexibility

When a company offers its employees flexibility in terms of workplaces and work hours, that's an example of trust and respect for individuals' needs. It's also recognition that it takes much more than only work in order for an individual to achieve his or her own level of excellence in work and in life.

Remember the WOW incident I mentioned earlier that had to do with my team member and her new convertible? Giving one employee a few hours off to enjoy her new car certainly didn't hurt the company, and it energized the employee and the work she did when she returned.

To Watch Or Not. Too many employers lack respect for their teams, and instead think that if they're not watching their employees every second, the work won't get done. If, indeed, the work won't get done without 24/7 monitoring of employees, there's something wrong with your company's culture and you have staffing issues that need to be addressed.

At one company, one of my team members was going through a horrific divorce. I knew she was terribly stressed, so I gave her the flexibility that she needed in her job. I trusted her to get the job done, and she did.

Our team rallied to help her with whatever she needed, including helping her move into a new home. Too few companies trust their people enough to make that kind of investment in them.

Not Easy But Essential. Flexibility isn't always easy, especially if your company has a regular set product. But some degree of flexibility is possible if a company's culture promotes its employees' working together as a team. Remember the US soldier wounded in Afghanistan? His mother was able to spend extended time with her son because her team at Allscripts stepped up to help cover her work.

We've all heard stories of a parent with a child who gets sick at school, and his or her employer balks at allowing the parent to leave work to take care of the child. Or, if the parent does leave, it's under a cloud of guilt perpetuated by the company's culture and ultimately its leadership. And what about the parent who fears his or her employer will find out he or she stayed home from work to take care of a sick child?

These scenarios are all unacceptable and yet far too common in today's workplace. Even with sales or service people who have demanding, time-sensitive jobs, teamwork can help address the needs in life. It's up to their companies and their leaders to remove the barriers, model the right culture, and help their teams cope.

That means fostering relationships with team members, treating them as the assets they are, and helping them manage situations. Time and again, great people burn out and quit their jobs because of an inflexible culture fostered by unenlightened leaders—people who don't understand the value of a flexible workplace. That happened to me early in my career. I handled the situation by launching my own business, but not everyone can do that successfully. Don't let it get to that point at your company.

Caring Gone Awry?

This past year, Yahoo!'s new CEO Marissa Mayer has been in the news for her abrupt move to end the company's flexible workplace policy. Now everyone has to work at the office.

Good leaders understand what truly motivates people. I absolutely believe that working as a team is the best way to achieve outcomes. But I don't believe a team has to be physically sitting together 100 percent of the time to reach those outcomes.

When people are motivated, they are able to be successful in their personal and business lives, and they will in turn achieve the greatest results for their companies. Instead of removing employees' workplace flexibility and limiting personal life success, a better approach to long-term success is to leverage technology. Add breadth to the come-together part of being a team and capitalize on teleconferencing, video conferencing, and more. Technology, after all, enables all of us to be our best.

Holding people accountable for results is what matters.

Caring Fosters Commitment

On a college trip with my daughter Danielle we visited the University of North Carolina-Wilmington (UNC-W). A typical high school senior at the time, Danielle wanted a hoodie from the school, so we went to the University Store. The cashier was an older woman—well into her retirement years, no matter who was counting. We began chatting, and it turned out she had been with the company 35 years.

"I can't leave," the white-haired septuagenarian told me. "I love it here. I'm a single mom, and I used to bring my child (she's now 30) here every day. It meant so much to me [back then] to have that flexibility to bring her here."

UNC-W got it right 30 years ago. They knew the importance of respect for their employees—including their personal lives.

The Power of Working Remotely

Not long ago, I came across a situation in which a Philadelphia-based company wanted to hire a top-notch marketing professional based in Austin, Texas.

The company had no presence in Austin, and the marketing expert, for personal reasons, could not relocate. But the company decided to accept her geographic limitations, and hired her anyway because of her branding talents.

After just six months in her new job, she's already generated positive results. Company brand recognition is way up.

Culture Check/Respect and Integrity

True integrity and respect can be an elusive goal in business. In many workplaces—I've mentioned a few in this chapter—executives and even line leaders may preach one thing, while in reality they practice the opposite.

A best-practice approach to help ensure that integrity and respect are part of the foundation of your company's culture demands open and honest discussions among leaders and teams. Often, individuals truly don't recognize when their actions or comments are disrespectful to others.

Begin by asking questions.

*What do integrity and respect mean to you?

*Can you give examples of both in your workplace?

*Can you give grievous examples of a lack of integrity and respect in your workplace?

*What about a subtle lack of both in your workplace?

Consider the following scenarios. Each reflects a lack of respect and/or integrity in a company. Do similar situations ever happen in your workplace? If so, what was the end result? What message did the actions convey to others in the company?

- *An employee gets a phone call at work from his daughter's school. The nine-year-old is being sent home because she's sick. When the father tells his boss that he has to leave to pick up the child and won't be back the rest of the day, the boss complains loudly about the extra work he's now forced to dump on others. After the father leaves, the negative conversation continues, too.*
- *A hard-working female employee is on the fast track to the top. All the opportunities come her way. Then she has a child, and although her performance remains top notch, suddenly the bosses look the other way when it comes to promotions and opportunities.*
- *A midlevel leader habitually is late to meetings with his team. Each time, he blames someone or something else.*

- *A single mom loses her regular babysitter for her toddler. She needs to find another sitter, so she asks her employer for some temporary workplace and time flexibility. Of course, she says that she'll get the same amount of work done. The employer denies her the flexibility, saying she has to be at work in the office every day at the regular time. "It's your problem. We're not a babysitting service, and don't want children in the office," the employer says.*
- *A female (or male) boss constantly flirts with the male (or female) hottie employee in the office. That same hottie seems to get all the plum assignments, and even when he/she makes mistakes, never gets reprimanded.*

We've all come across similar situations in various workplaces. Talk about how in each instance, specific behavior modifications might enhance the level of integrity and respect at your company. What can leadership do to better model the expected value?

Think about how your company handles layoffs and/or firings.

Is the company honest about the situation and fair in its treatment of those employees facing job loss? Or does it take the more typical attitude of "Here's your pink slip. Don't let the door hit you in the back as you leave"?

Most often, it's somewhere in the middle. You'll get a week or two of severance, but not much more and certainly with the attitude of a minimum of disruption for the company. Only the very best companies recognize the payback that comes from truly caring.

CHAPTER 5

Innovation: It's Not Complicated

Make things better, or make better things.

—*Diane K. Adams*

What's the very best way to make something happen? That's the question successful companies, their leaders, and employees ask and answer every day as they strengthen their long-term success. And that's what a culture that promotes innovation in the workplace is all about.

A Different Kind of Thinking

Innovation is a competitive differentiator. It's about thinking big and differently. Ben and Jerry of ice cream fame weren't afraid of creating a socially responsible business—an almost unheard of concept when they started out in the 1970s.

Innovation is also about thinking ahead. Glen Tullman, CEO of Allscripts from 1997 to 2012, recognized that technology could offer a better way of keeping medical records than rows of paper files. He took the chance on innovative change, and it netted his company billions of dollars.

On a smaller scale, in 2001 Buck Buchanan was determined to interest North Carolinians in healthy ice cream. Despite the recession, he launched his business, Lumpy's. With his innovative product and approach—home-style, fresh, and healthy ice cream, along with personal production and delivery in a crowded and impersonal market—he became a regional success.

None of these leaders was afraid to be different or to think big. They didn't allow roadblocks to stand in the way of growing their businesses and their industries, either.

Simple Solutions

Innovations don't have to be complex. Like some of the world's top executives, these men recognized that simplicity can drive innovation.

Zappos! CEO Tony Hsieh had a laser focus on customer service. He wrote a book in which he talks about that customer service and its importance in a company's culture, (*Delivering Happiness: A Path to Profits, Passion, and Purpose,* Business Plus, 2010). His thoughts on customer service are legendary: "Zappos is a customer service company that just happens to sell shoes."

The success of Zappos! is online retailing history. Even after the company's 2009 purchase by giant Amazon.com, the company's No. 1 core value remains, "Deliver WOW through service."[1]

Zappos! on developing its customer base through "WOW" service: "To WOW, you must differentiate yourself, which means doing something a little unconventional and innovative.... Our philosophy at Zappos is to WOW with service and experience, not with anything that relates directly to monetary compensation (for example, we don't offer blanket discounts or promotions to customers)."[2]

Another leader who focuses on simplicity is Charlie Giancarlo, a former technology leader at Cisco, and now a venture capitalist (managing partner, SilverLake). During his tenure at Cisco, he streamlined research and development.

Instead of multiple layers of bureaucracy and presentations typically associated with new products and design, Giancarlo made sure his developers could immediately access the right individuals and organizations for their projects and products. Designers, therefore, were able to concentrate on design, and not get bogged down by layers of bureaucracy.

Giancarlo's point was that you'll never have a culture of innovation—thinking creatively—if you're bogged down in too much process.

In Search of a "Better Way"

Both men weren't afraid to think about a better way of doing things. They understood that a culture that embraces innovation can drive success. Like Tullman, Buchanan, and Ben and Jerry, they understood the secret of simplicity.

Dean Kamen is probably best known for his invention of the Segway, an electric upright human transporter. It didn't catch on as big as developers had expected, but it definitely was an innovative alternative form of two-wheeled transport.

Kamen has a long list of other inventions that all start with innovation and the concept of finding a better way to do something. Among those inventions are an implantable insulin pump, an all-terrain electric wheelchair, and a nonpolluting low-power water purifying system.[3]

Innovation at Nonprofits

I joined the board of directors of the Juvenile Diabetes Research Foundation (JDRF) at a time when diabetes research costs had soared. We needed to accelerate our fundraising efforts.

With my background in innovation as a driver for success, we are developing innovative ways to raise money and reward donors. We've had successful Virtual Walks (for diabetes research). We recorded a Rap Sent 'Round the World on YouTube, and our newest innovation is the One Walk program to raise the bar on our funding.

JDRF's fundraising has soared. Since its inception in 1970, JDRF has raised $1.7 billion for research.

Innovation in Small Businesses

Innovation must play a role in every company. It's especially relevant for small businesses in the face of stiff competition from mega corporations. North Carolina's Lumpy's Ice Cream took to Facebook to scoop the competition by broadening its reach and connecting with loyal customers.

Innovation also means the vision to see beyond the status quo. In fact, experts today talk about vision and innovation as essential roles of a small business owner. Without it, a business simply can't compete long term with what increasingly are becoming global competitors.

Lumpy's founder and chief ice cream maker Buchanan's goal was to make affordable healthy ice cream with farm-fresh and hand-cut ingredients. He sold that ice cream out of a food truck. It was an innovative business model when the company began more than a decade ago. "Our business model is now the 'norm,'" says Buchanan. "Now you see tons of ice cream trucks and food trucks."

A relative newcomer that's all about innovation is digedu. The Chicago-based technology company focuses on transitioning schools from textbooks to technology-based learning. Already it's an idea that's been successful with a number of school districts in the United States.

Digedu's platform includes plug-and-play technology with devices, software, and services that offer interactive, individually tailored, self-paced learning instruction at a fraction of the cost of traditional textbooks. Savings based on national averages are $350 to $600 per student per year, according to Lee Shapiro, chairman of digedu's board of directors, a managing partner at 7wire Ventures, and former president of Allscripts.

This different approach to education is about leveling the academic playing field, giving everyone the opportunity and wherewithal to learn. That's innovation.

The Challenge

Too often, business leaders and owners reject the idea of innovation with the typical comment "If it's not broken, why fix it?" In other words, why challenge the status quo? It's always been done that way; it works, so why change? Why even bother to think about change?

No matter how you frame these short-sighted questions, the answer is simple: so that you don't watch the competition pass you by.

Innovation is an important survival tool, says Carlos Dominguez, internationally recognized innovations guru. "In a world changing so rapidly, the only way to survive is to constantly innovate and re-invent."

Carlos told me that he once asked Procter & Gamble CEO A. G. Lafley what kept him up at night—what worried him the most? Lafley responded that, with his 40 years in the packaged-goods industry, he worried that he may see problems in today's new business world in the old way!

That's the response of a true leader who recognizes the importance of innovation.

We know innovation matters. Yet, it's a tough challenge when it comes to following through, especially since so many companies often prefer to rely on what's made them successful in the past rather than recognize the fast obsolescence of past actions.

The Vision

Times change, and businesses and their leaders must have the vision to plan for the future. Think about the banking industry, for example, and how it has been transformed since the Internet. Banks have gone from local branch-centric to having a huge digital presence. In fact, without vision and innovative ideas for dealing with the future, a financial institution can't compete successfully in today's evolving environment.

That's a reality not lost on Pittsburgh-based PNC Financial Services Group's Chairman, President, and CEO William Demchak. In fact, Bill talked about the importance of vision at the 2014 North Carolina CEO Forum, an annual event I co-host in Raleigh.

"The world is changing around me," he told an audience of corporate leaders. "We know we need to deal with it. We've seen what happens to companies who don't deal with it. Think about what happened with Blockbuster Video..."

Embracing Change

Long-term successful companies operate with the innovation question constantly in mind. Their people always ask themselves, what's the absolute newest and best way to achieve the goal/goals?

Whether the goal involves an external or internal concept, procedure, policy, product, service, or something else, companies that look for how to do it better for the future aren't afraid of change. They embrace it, and they usually succeed.

Earlier I mentioned some of the "little things" Strata Decisions CEO Dan Michelson did to improve things at his company. His approach included issuing paychecks weekly rather than monthly. The company's long-term policy of monthly paychecks wasn't necessarily broken. But, based on employee feedback, employees weren't happy with the policy.

The best and simplest way to achieve the goal of happy employees was to compensate them weekly. Michelson took this simple action and changed the policy. Having more satisfied employees was worth the small extra cost of producing additional checks.

The 90 Percent Equation

No matter what the goal, I think in terms of the statement "What is the simplest, most effective way to get from Point A to Point Z?" The answer isn't always a 100 percent solution. But by looking for simple and innovative solutions, and weighing the pros and cons of the different possibilities, as a leader you arrive at the most effective choice for reaching your goal—to arrive at Point Z from Point A.

In the case of Strata Decisions, changing the frequency of employee compensation was a simple way to create a majority of happier employees. Innovative leaders recognize that sometimes a 90 percent solution to a goal equates to success.

Michelson's move, too, was even more effective because at the same time, his action conveyed to employees that the company really does care, and as a part of that, listens to its employees.

Simplification Can Save Cash

No matter your position or the job you do in a company, you, too, should think about the simplest and best way to achieve an outcome. That's especially true when it comes to processes.

As Giancarlo taught me, often processes are far too complex and cumbersome, and stymie innovation rather than encourage it. Simplifying processes can cut down on costs, as well.

The Business of Performance Evaluations. As a people expert, I handle employee evaluations as part of my job. Continually I find companies using complex, confusing, and expensive performance evaluation procedures. In fact, performance evaluation itself is a thriving multibillion-dollar business.

With innovation, processes, and procedures in mind, though, do you really need 15 steps to evaluate someone's performance in his or her job? Do multiple employees and managers really need to be involved to get a solid picture of an individual's performance? And do you need to spend thousands or hundreds of thousands, or even millions of dollars on elaborate software and systems to get a fair and accurate performance review?

I prefer an innovative, simple, and more cost-effective approach—three solid steps to performance evaluation: employee feedback, manager and employee conversations, and manager evaluations.

De-motivator. Too often, getting your leadership to produce employee evaluations is tough. They never have time. But there's an easy solution. Not only is a complex employee-evaluation system time consuming, but it's also a demotivator. Innovate and simplify instead, and the results will surprise you.

Some big companies like Microsoft Corporation (Nasdaq: MSFT) and Juniper Networks (NYSE: JNPR) actually are moving away from performance ratings of their employees. They recognize that when the process becomes so complex, you actually can lose sight of the initial intent of performance management systems—to provide valuable feedback so that the performance of an employee, his or her leader, and ultimately the company improves and thrives.

Short and to the Point. Even though Cisco is a multibillion-dollar operation, early on John Chambers set the mark when it comes to performance evaluations. The evaluations were one page in length, with bulleted comments that cover four areas of personal performance:

*accomplishments for the previous year

*priorities for the next year

*assessment of strengths

*areas on which to focus personal learning in the coming year

Other companies need to emulate this approach. It turns evaluations into the conversations they should be.

How to Create an Innovative Culture

Creating a culture of innovation doesn't have to be difficult. The best ideas come from talking. Whether your company or team is large, small or in-between, take the time to brainstorm and listen.

Innovative companies invest the time and energy into brainstorming—enabling multiple inputs to solve a problem or reach a goal—to make sure they're making, doing, or acting in the best, most effective and efficient manner.

Without pausing to think about *it*—whatever *it* is—all you have is concept and execution.

Talk Is Cheap!

More can be better when it comes to innovation. While I was at Allscripts, rather than pay tens of thousands of dollars to a single developer to try to come up with new product innovations, we created a platform for innovation, a series of innovation challenges for outside developers and vendors. That meant, instead of one person or one mind working to build a better mousetrap, we looked to dozens of minds to create and integrate applications that could be extensions of Allscripts' software.

For example, the Open App Challenge, issued in October 2012, offered awards for apps "focused on the management of high cost chronic diseases and value-based care imperatives," according to an Allscripts press release. The contest included $750,000 in total awards, with the overall winner taking home $250,000. "We want the smartest people, whether physicians, nurses, caregivers or IT professionals inside and outside the industry to use their creative energy to solve real problems in healthcare," CEO Tullman said at the time.

The challenge was a big success, with almost 100 developers participating. The company Healthfinch won first place, with its Refill wizard application that automates prescription renewal requests.[4]

Innovation Leader on Staff

Cisco is so serious about the importance of innovation that John appointed an innovation ambassador to travel the globe and talk about the culture of innovation.

Smaller companies may not need a globetrotter to promote a culture of innovation, but they could appoint their own innovation meister, someone whose task revolves around making sure innovation is part of everyday life in the company. That sends a clear message to everyone in the company about the importance of thinking and doing with innovation in mind.

Listening Forums

Another way to tap the creativity of multiple minds is through listening forums. No matter how large or small a company, an all-hands meeting or series of meetings that encourage discussions—that's what a listening forum is—can be a great way to brainstorm for solutions to a problem or to find a better way to do something.

At Qlik, brainstorming sessions also have been invaluable sources of innovation. We wanted to step up our peer recognition, for example, but were unsure of the best approach to generate interest. From our listening forums came the idea of also recognizing employees who nominated their peers. Recognition included a book on the value of rewarding employees, along with a note of thanks from their boss. Within three weeks, we had 140 people recognized for demonstrating their values.

All Inclusive. Our brainstorming at Qlikinvolves everyone, from the boss to the employees. It can be the same at your company, too.

Because Qlik has grown so fast, we were concerned about losing personal connections among all the employees. In a brainstorming session, one employee suggested that everyone should include their individual photo as the norm in signing e-mails. We took the concept of names linked with faces a step further, requiring video conference calls.

Now, if I'm sitting in my office in Pennsylvania and get an email from someone in Sweden whom I don't know personally, I at least know what that person looks like. I can connect on a more personal level because I have a face with a name.

It's OK to have fun with the pictures, too. One colleague regularly switches her photo, and even used Sandra Bullock's picture. This is just like switching your profile picture on Facebook. The point, though, is the same. It's about developing personal relationships with others.

Easy to Do. Any company and its employees—yours included—can and should sit down, talk, and listen. That's what brainstorming is—talking and listening.

Raleigh-based Rachel Kendall Realty, which I mentioned earlier, does this all the time—every week, and then quarterly, all team members meet off-site to talk and listen. They brainstorm about the guiding principles that create their culture; their goals and where they are with their goals; and how they can help each other achieve those goals, says Rachel Kendall.

How important is the brainstorming? It's an essential part of nurturing and growing a company's culture. In the case of Kendall's company, it's small, but has a very strong team culture.

"The biggest thing is we care about the team," says Kendall. You can't teach intrinsic values, but you can nurture them, she says. Talking and listening to each other is part of that. "We enjoy brainstorming; it's fun...it's our team."

The T-shirt Equation

During my tenure at Allscripts, CEO Tullman's measure of our innovation at any given time was the number of new T-shirts we had printed.

As wild as that metric sounds, it was a solid measure because whenever a team came up with a new innovation, we had T-shirts printed to promote the cool new idea or approach. Team members loved it. The T-shirts fueled enthusiasm, and they promoted the innovation, idea, and/or accomplishment.

At my current company, Qlik, our growth has been meteoric. In 2012, we were the fastest growing technology company in the United States behind Apple and LinkedIn. To help promote the cohesive, team culture that's always been Qlik, we had T-shirts printed with various slogans related to our products. They were a huge success.

It's not a complicated promotional approach or costly. And, of course, printed T-shirts alone don't ensure cohesive integration companywide. But it's something special and different, and helps convey the importance of our company's culture.

While I was at Cisco, every year the company participated in JDRF's Walk for the Cure. Every year we designed a special T-shirt that was worn by our walk teams, too.

The same thing happened at Allscripts. This time, though, the children of employees submitted designs for the T-shirts. Winners—we picked several—received prizes. One year, a winner even donated her $100 prize from Allscripts to the JDRF cause.

Culture Check/Innovation

Now it's time to assess your company's attitude and approach toward innovation and change. It's time to ask the hard questions and deal with the honest answers.

Is your company's leader willing to think big and differently? Does he or she have a vision for the future? If so, does it involve change in some way? The vision could be to become a bigger company or a better one in some way or ways. Or, it could involve both.

Alternatively, a leader's vision could involve the status quo – no change is good. Unfortunately, that's not a solid approach for any business today. Without continual innovation in today's constantly changing environment, a business actually falls behind.

What is your company's attitude toward innovation?

- *Does it encourage employees to think of a better way to do things? Or is the boss' way the only way? Remember, success is a team effort!*
- *How do the company and its leadership handle suggestions from others? Are suggestions automatically rejected, or do they have a chance to be studied, understood, and possibly implemented? Of course, the right answer is the latter.*
- *Does the company hand out kudos for new and better approaches within the company's stated values? That's part of the formula for long-term growth and success.*

Do your company and its leaders formally foster innovation? Does the company have a platform that promotes open listening forums to give everyone the opportunity to offer input? These interactive sessions don't have to be called "listening forums." They can be all-hands meetings or smaller groups that get together. At Rachel Kendall Realty, for example, these are weekly meetings. Another option for a small business could be to hold a once-a-month coffee gathering.

Whatever the format, though, these sessions should be regular, scheduled, all inclusive, and promote open back-and-forth discussions and interactions. They provide an opportunity to offer suggestions on better ways of doing things; they keep all hands aware of the company's current VSEs; and they promote camaraderie.

Don't overlook follow-up on the ideas and discussions in these sessions. It's simply not enough to listen, and then forget or overlook. Concrete follow-up on discussions is important, not only as an indicator that the company listens and cares but also in recognizing the value that each of its team members brings to the table.

Keep in mind that many of these innovative ideas do impact the bottom line.

CHAPTER 6

Listen More Than Talk: Communications and Collaboration Are Essential

Company success is a team sport.

—*Diane K. Adams*

S ustainable success is a group effort. In a successful business, everyone is a contributor and a collaborator. That's why long-term winning companies think about their employees and leaders as a team whose members work together toward common goals.

We're in This Together!

Great companies embrace this kind of open collaboration, while others choose to ignore it, whether from fear, insecurity, or the belief that it's more important to concentrate on profits. No surprise, though, profits are a direct result of a team that truly collaborates and communicates.

Collaboration in the workplace means two-way talking and listening across all levels from the top tier to the bottom tier, between leaders and employees, among employees and customers, and customers and leaders. It's two-way discussion and criticism, open feedback without fear of repercussions, two-way performance reviews, and more.

Results Are the Proof

In the last chapter, I mentioned Rachel Kendall Realty, with which I've had the pleasure of working personally and professionally. Not only does its namesake owner recognize the role of culture in her company's success, but she also nurtures a team environment that is all about communications and collaboration.

Real estate is a tough business. Competition between agents is fierce. Leads on new listings are high value, and typically only shared for a price—usually a percentage of the sale. Except at team Rachel Kendall.

"We work together to help each other achieve our goals," says Rachel. "We absolutely share leads with each other. We don't charge percentages for those leads, either, because we work as a team. . . . Everyone is in this together."

That's why Rachel Kendall is so successful and leaves its competition in the dust.

Not Always Smooth Sailing

Any kind of success, though, isn't without its rough patches. I worked with another service provider that asked its employees to rate their bosses as a way to help identify weak areas of the organization and begin to lay the foundation for improvement.

Almost all the managers welcomed the feedback and were anxious to change for the better. One middle manager, though, seriously balked. He had a reputation for an uneven and unfair management style. He regularly showed favoritism and dispensed criticism arbitrarily.

Yet, when confronted with his faults, as often happens, he chose to take the feedback as constructive criticism from his team members, and make the changes necessary to cement success.

An Evolving Process

As is typical with companies—large or small—in their early years, management takes a command-and-control approach. That's what happened at Cisco. In the beginning, leaders took charge and gave direction. Then came the company's meteoric growth.

Then-CEO John Chambers recognized that this command-and-control management style was not the way to successfully scale the company. He knew that creating a collaborative environment was.

Building in Incentives. To help encourage that behavior, leadership began to pay attention to how well each employee collaborated within and outside his or her teams to get the desired results. Peer feedback on employee collaboration became an integral part of standard performance reviews.

Admittedly, for the first year or so, most employees sugarcoated the truth about their peers. But by the second or third year of the program, as people realized the company was committed to real collaboration, employees began honestly to assess each other's collaborative skills.

Getting the Results. The thinking shifted to open and honest communications and follow-up to do what was necessary to get the right results.

This change didn't happen overnight. But with the guidance of leaders intentionally modeling the right behavior—the expected actions—Cisco transitioned to its desired collaborative environment.

It's OK to Have Doubts. On the subject of honest communications, early in my tenure at Cisco, I wasn't a fan of that kind of peer feedback, especially as a measure of real collaboration. I was concerned that as a company we would end up with sugarcoated comments from employees.

But I later realized how wrong my initial reaction had been, as we began truly getting honest and constructive feedback. Cisco at the time went from a just-get-it-done culture to one in which team members always asked who needed to be involved in a particular project to get it done optimally. Reaching out to peers became automatic, plus we began recognizing people for their expertise.

When It Works

We take a similar approach at Qlik. Individuals are recognized throughout the company for their special skills. That makes it clear who or which team has the expertise that may be required to get something done right.

The bottom line, after all, is about collaboration and a shift from the just-get-it-done culture to one that strives for excellence and to complete a goal in the very best way possible.

From Entrepreneurial to Established

A company can't grow its way out of trouble. Instead, it takes vision, goals, and strategies to get there. Too few organizations recognize that until it's too late.

Scaling a Culture

Entrepreneurial companies often grow quickly and end up grappling with what to do next. That's because their early culture, as in processes and guidelines, which worked initially often can't scale as the company grows. With success, a company's culture must evolve from just make it happen to one that teaches people how to partner across an organization, to collaborate, and to communicate.

When I joined Qlik, a priority was to maintain what had always been its truly open communications. The company had grown so quickly—from 850 to 1,700 people in two years—that maintaining the open communications had become a seemingly insurmountable task. Lars, a strong proponent of open communications and collaboration, brought me on board to help develop a process to successfully scale the company's culture.

Lars especially wanted to stay connected with his sales organization, now spread out across the world. One of the first things we did was set up listening forums. Utilizing technology links, Lars met with 15 of the top sales leaders to discuss current sales opportunities as well as his vision for the future. This inclusive meeting was a first for the company, and these savvy sales leaders recognized its importance. They also knew that the meeting provided them an opportunity to connect and communicate directly with the CEO. They even prepared for the meeting ahead of time by getting together on their own time to prioritize what they wanted to discuss.

One of the top topics of discussion was Lars' vision for the company's future. These leaders needed a clear picture of where the company was going so that they could in turn paint a compelling vision for their own teams, too.

Small Companies Sometimes Struggle, Too

Almost anyone and any company can struggle with open and ongoing communications. It happens to the best of leaders and the strongest companies.

Remember SEPI Engineering and its leader, Sepi Saidi, that I mentioned earlier? The successful engineering firm is all about two-way communications and collaboration. Sepi solicits and expects input from her employees and vice versa.

Sepi told me a story about hiring an industry veteran a few years ago who was unaccustomed to a boss who solicited and listened to her input. Shocked by Sepi's "out-of-the ordinary" behavior, the employee initially hesitated to speak up. Having worked for other bosses who said they wanted feedback, but really didn't care what she had to say, the employee feared repercussions for expressing her opinions.

Sepi had to sit down one-on-one with the woman and talk to her about her company's team-oriented culture. Every employee, she told her, is a valuable team member whose input is a crucial part of the company's long-term growth and success.

Since then, the now devoted employee has learned to let her voice be heard. She's become an essential member of the team and recognizes the company is better for her contributions—positive and negative.

Pervasive and Intentional

Communications and collaboration can't be arbitrary or a pick-and-choose kind of thing, either, in any business. It's built into a culture, and therefore is pervasive in all aspects and actions of that business.

Celebration Turned Sour

A San Francisco-based international service provider faced sizable layoffs in order to streamline its operations. Its CEO planned a big party to honor those employees and their accomplishments.

Recognizing these peoples' contributions was a great idea. Unfortunately, though, the initiative came up short. (Remember my admonition mentioned earlier: be careful of what you do when everyone is watching.) Some employees quietly complained about the company's holding a party at a time when others were losing their jobs.

The Missing Piece. Despite the CEO's best intentions, he had overlooked two-way discussions on the party idea. He didn't get input from all stakeholders—both the existing as well as the departing employees. He also didn't thoroughly explain to everyone the reasons behind the layoffs, and why the company could afford the party, but could not retain the employees. Nor did he give those exiting employees an opportunity to offer their ideas on what might be the best way to celebrate their years of loyalty to the company.

Another Viewpoint. The end result of this communications breakdown on both sides was that not all employees understood that a party is a one-time, minimal, and affordable expense, as opposed to the long-term costs of an FTE—full-time equivalent employee. The end result was disgruntled employees.

A Better Approach. Had the CEO been more open with employees and instead asked for and listened to their input on how to honor the soon-to-be-let-go individuals, he could have avoided the negative backlash.

At the San Francisco company, the backlash was minimal, but at other companies it's not always that simple.

Unilateral Decision-making

Another common mistake that torpedoes open communications is unilateral decision-making by the boss. That's especially common with compensation issues at all kinds and sizes of companies. The boss, for example, needs to be thoughtful and thorough in making compensation decisions as opposed to arbitrarily deciding who does or doesn't get raises or bonuses.

He or she may be the boss, but in the case of compensation, rubrics must be established; employees' performance must be measured or be based on those rubrics; and then achievements must be rewarded based on performance.

Without that approach and the all-important two-way communications on performance, employees and leaders don't really know what's expected of them and can't successfully set their goals in line with the company's goals.

Communications Drives Success

At the other end of the spectrum, Allscripts recognized the power of good communications and made all the right moves to ensure its success.

The company's growth was exploding. The health-care technology pioneer had just made two major global acquisitions, and worried that it would lose its edge if it couldn't maintain the cohesive, team-oriented culture that had sustained it.

Process to Scale

My team was charged with making it all work. To achieve that, my team, led by Richard Byrd, created a communications process that could scale to include everyone. That meant everyone could be heard, their comments and feedback understood, and actions taken. My team also coached leaders on how to convey clear expectations to every employee every step of the way. It wasn't easy. But it worked.

For example, to make sure employees understood what was expected of them, everyone new went through a real orientation, not the typical gloss-over kind. We took the time to meet with each individual to explain the company's culture, its history, vision, and mission/impact, and to train them about our products and their individual jobs.

We emphasized that we wanted every person to be successful and play to his or her strengths, which is why every employee completed a strength assessment upfront.

Good Connections

Allscripts was committed to truly listening to its employees globally, too. Lee Shapiro, then company president, knew the power of connecting with employees as well as customers.

Throughout India, for example, we regularly met with team members in various cities. Each time, Lee would begin his presentations in the native language. That created an instant connection with the audience.

Small Gesture/Big Gains. In a culture in which people often are reserved and hesitant to speak out and share their ideas, we found this small gesture made a big difference in the openness of employees and their leaders.

We would leave these meetings with valuable feedback on a variety of issues. We followed up on those issues, too.

All-Important Follow-Up. At one of these meetings, several employees raised concerns about the company's travel policy and how it differed between India and the United States. It turned out that US-based employees flying to India flew business class with more spacious seating, while those flying from India to the United States were required to fly coach.

We immediately changed the policy so that anyone flying more than six hours went business class. What had been an inadvertent inequity in company policy was corrected.

Key Piece Often Missing

Too often, companies—big, small, and in-between—solicit feedback. But they overlook or ignore the follow-up, and lose the respect of their team members as a result.

You don't have to be an international corporate superstar like Shapiro to make the effort to listen to and act on your employees' or your customers' feedback. But you do have to be willing to hear what's said, take it to heart, and care about resolving problems or issues. That's the spirit of real communications, collaboration, and long-term success.

HOW COMMUNICATIONS HELPED ALLSCRIPTS DEVELOP ITS TEAM CULTURE

Allscripts helped make sure its entire company understood its culture, in part by focusing on clear and open communications across all levels of the company. To achieve that, the company took actions that included:

- *quarterly leadership meetings held by each leader, starting with the CEO;*
- *quarterly all-hands meetings to provide direction, updates, and recognition;*
- *listening forums with 10 to 15 people, the CEO or Executive, and the author (as the Culture and Talent expert) for the purpose of listening to what was working and what needed to be changed, which included follow-up to concerns, feedback, and comments;*
- *minimum biweekly staff meetings held by all leaders;*
- *minimum biweekly one-on-one meetings between leaders and team members; and*
- *leadership training, including an annual face-to-face meeting with the senior leadership team to provide clear direction and relevant training/education for the coming year.*

Power of Two-Way Communications

At Strata Decisions, CEO Dan Michelson requires his employees to rate his performance anonymously. He expects them to do so honestly, without any repercussions, and he listens to what they say, and acts on it. He even shares the feedback with his board of directors.

A perfect example of that is the company's switch to weekly paychecks as opposed to monthly that I mentioned earlier. The shift was the direct result of employee feedback.

Cisco's Chambers also subscribes to that kind of two-way communications. To help manage the volume of feedback that he receives from tens of thousands of employees worldwide, he established Birthday Breakfasts. On an employee's birthday, he or she could ask John any question. Through the years—the breakfast-question approach began in 1995—he's been asked everything from why the company changed its compensation policies, to why the stock isn't moving, to why health-care costs for employees are going up, to why the company stopped offering free drinks to employees. The questions and the actions taken—John's responses and the leaderships' actions—are posted online. Employee response to the question of free beverages was so great that it crashed the company's email.

Cisco listened to its employees and made the changes. The free beverage policy was reinstated.

Hiring Fit

Communications and collaboration extend to a company, making sure that new hires are the right fit with the company's culture.

Hiring mistakes, after all, cost money—the cost of training, relocation, and more. The wrong hire also can upset the delicate team balance. That's one reason top companies rely on multiple interviews before ever hiring someone.

I had 27 interviews with Cisco before they hired me. That's not a typo—27 interviews. That's a lot of interviews—probably more of an investment than most companies are willing to make. But John wanted to be absolutely certain I was the right culture fit, especially since my role there would center on promoting and perpetuating the culture. At the time, the company was expanding by 100 new hires every week.

Cisco's hiring guidelines stipulated a minimum of seven interviews, and the entire interview team had to be in agreement before any new hire. That may be why I had so many interviews. John and his team wanted to make sure I had a strong team-oriented approach to solving problems. John insisted on multiple interviews to ensure a culture fit with all his employees, no exceptions. Shortly after the policy began, he asked an orientation session of 100 people, who has not had seven interviews? Five people raised their hands. After the meeting, he spoke with each of those five individuals' leaders and explained his expectations. That was the last time anyone was hired with fewer than the minimum number of interviews.

Culture fit is essential with small businesses, too. With an eye on expansion, Rachel Kendall recently interviewed 30 agents in one week. Most were great producers, but she hired only one person. Only one individual was a good fit for her team. Remember, Rachel's company's culture is all about communications and collaboration among her team members. She—or any business—can't afford to bring in anyone who doesn't subscribe to open communications and collaboration—who isn't a willing team player.

"I would rather have someone with no experience, than someone who wasn't a good culture fit," she says. "The problem is, people say they are all about culture, but then they deviate from it when they see someone who can produce more money for the company."

Focus on the "We," Not the "Me"

Like Kendall's team approach, only the best companies focus on what the company, its leaders, and its employees can do together. Instead, it's about what they can't do and about the "me." That's a big disconnect that makes a big difference.

The Disconnect

Many times throughout my career I've encountered companies with people who focused on strong individual results, instead of focusing on the team. It was a "me" as opposed to a "we" mentality.

In those situations, jealousies can fester, and staffing becomes an expensive revolving door. Long-term company success simply doesn't happen either.

I remember one staffing situation in which a boss and his employee complemented each other. The employee was smart and strategy-oriented compared with his HR chief, who was relationship-oriented and excelled at reaching out to work with others. Together, they would have made a great team. Instead, though, rather than capitalizing on each other's strengths, the boss tried to undermine his employee with poor performance reviews. Fortunately, the employee's outstanding performance was well documented with positive feedback from other employees and department heads. The end result was the boss was fired.

No Room for Jealousies and Egomaniacs

My philosophy is one of abundance—there's enough success to go around for everyone.

Unfortunately, some people instead are focused on the "me."

Often, it's the result of their own insecurities. That can destroy a great place to work.

Making the Right Choice. In a situation like that, you make the decision—either they go or you go.

One phenomenal leader at a technology company called me recently to share his unfortunate story. He had left a top job with excellent financial benefits to work for another leader who he thought was really strong. Despite the cut in pay he took for the new job, he had been excited and optimistic.

At the new job he immediately bonded with his team members. They rated his leadership as tops, while his new boss received dismal ratings. The boss became so jealous that my friend had to quit the company. He was forced to make the decision to walk away. The next day—no surprise—four of his team members quit, too.

In a perfect world, the jealous boss should have been the one to go. But as we all see too often in our imperfect world, that's not what usually happens.

For the Team. Your company's success should be a proactive demonstration of what each of your people brings to the workplace, says Rachel Kendall.

She's absolutely right. If you truly lay the foundation for communications and collaboration, your people know that what they do is important, that they're recognized for their contributions, and they will feel like they're an essential part of a team organization. All that can go a long way toward eliminating jealousies, which can poison an organization.

Meetings and Communicating

How many times have you or someone you know walked out of or skipped a staff meeting, saying, "It's a waste of time." Staff meetings at successful companies are NOT a waste of time. Nor should they be in an organization that is based on true communications and collaboration.

High Value

Done right, meetings of any kind are informational, educational, and a valuable opportunity to exchange information and ideas. Their focus should be on what everyone can do, not what they can't, whether individually or as a team.

Forget reading off written remarks. Even a regular staff meeting should be a proactive, interactive discussion. Remember, communications is a two-way interchange of ideas.

Actions and Expectations

Staff meetings should be held at least bi-weekly and absolutely include substantive issues like expectations of actions aligned with specific goals. As I discussed earlier, when everyone's actions are aligned toward the same goals, a company's growth can accelerate.

Rachel Kendall huddles daily with her team. The company's performance reflects the value of that kind of communications.

Every Monday morning at Qlik, the leadership team gets together for a 30-minute round-table discussion of what everyone is doing that week. As a result, all employees know what everyone else is working on for the week and their priorities.

The meetings also further enhance our team approach to achieving goals quickly and efficiently. For example, at one recent meeting I discovered that a teammate had a scheduled meeting with a potential customer who is a hospital executive with whom I've worked previously. Since I already understand the executive's decision-making, I followed up with the team member outside our general meeting to share my expertise. That's true collaboration and teamwork. It likely wouldn't have happened, either, without our weekly Monday information exchanges.

Key Ingredients—Meeting in a Box!

No matter the agenda, every staff meeting also has key ingredients, which include

- a business update—what's top-of-mind for the company at the moment; this could include key messages from senior leaders;
- team priorities and updates on the status of accomplishing those goals; and
- what's top-of-mind for your team.

To ensure these essentials are covered at our meetings, we regularly send out what I call a **Meeting in a Box (MIAB)**. This an electronic outline/meeting guide containing details of what's important now in the company, an explanation of what the executive team is doing, clear expectations of deliverables, and status on achievement of goals, plus anything else that's important and current.

An MIAB also could include mention of specific projects that need to be examined. This isn't micromanaging. Instead, it's laying the groundwork to keep teams focused on deliverables within the stated time frames.

With an MIAB you also reinforce alignment of actions company wide, with the result of less wasted time and effort, and faster deliverables.

Don't forget at the end of each meeting to recap actions from the meeting as well as to agree on what the priorities are for discussion at the next meeting. Follow up on your meetings, too. That means internal notes to leaders and/or team members detailing the important issues discussed and goals set.

Integrating Values

Think of meetings of any kind as a time to reinforce company values.

For example, all-hands meetings should include slides and related discussions about the company's core values. At Cisco, Allscripts, and now at Qlik, the content of our all-hands meetings included PowerPoint slides that review company values. We have also discussed how team members were doing in relation to those values—what they're doing right and what they need to do in the future to improve how we live those values.

Even individual communications with employees should refer to relevant company values. For example, if you're in an update meeting with an employee, and a company value is customer service, take the time to praise that employee's behavior that aligns with the company's values. Talk about ways in which the employee can enhance his or her performance, too.

Two-Way Communications and Engagement

Kudos don't always have to be formal awards. A short comment on a job well done at the bottom of a memo goes a long way toward helping team members know they're appreciated.

Often, companies and their leaders may know employees are doing a good job, but aren't sure of the right way to provide the "atta boy" or "atta girl." The engagement portion is missing.

At Qlik, we work hard to recognize peer performance that aligns with the company's values. Not long ago, the team came up with a unique way to do so. We sent a message to leaders asking for peer nominations and providing a URL on which to post the kudos. Within two hours, 41 individuals already had been recognized for a job well done.

Make the Connection

Connecting with your audience—whether it's a one-on-one discussion or a speech to a big audience—is another important component that enhances the ability to communicate.

Along with that engagement comes the importance of relevance.

Personal Connections

While I was at Allscripts, I frequently began my speeches, whether to industry or company employees or customers, with a bit of personal background:

> *"I'm Diane Adams, I've been in the health-care field for many years. My daughter has Type I diabetes, so I've spent plenty of time in lots of different hospitals and health-care settings."*

As simple as those lines were, they created a connection to the audience. The audience knew I wasn't just another executive. I became human, and they knew that I understood their business.

Do Your Homework

Take the time to know your audience. Who are they? What's their background? How might you make the personal connection? Do your homework.

I find academic backgrounds—where you or audience members attended college, for example—can be a great way to make the connection. I had scheduled a meeting that I knew would be difficult, with an executive who had a reputation for being tough and unapproachable. While preparing for the meeting, I noticed that he was a graduate of Duke University. That's an arch-rival of my alma mater, the University of North Carolina.

To help connect with him, I started out the meeting by saying, "You're a graduate of Duke; I'm a UNC grad, but we won't let the rivalry get in the way, for now!"

That comment was enough to break the ice, to connect, and to enhance our ability to really communicate with each other.

Culture Check/Communications and Collaboration

Open communications and collaboration are essential in a positive values-based culture with a strong team that fosters long-term success.

Are open communications and collaboration the norm at your company? I'm talking about the idea of communicating as more than just empty words without actions that back them up. Too often, leaders say they run a business that promotes communications, but in reality they ignore or even penalize someone for speaking up. That includes customers. In other words, the company operates in a culture of "my way or the highway!"

Too many companies and their leaders say they favor communications, but that means perhaps once a year (or less often) all-hands meetings or group get-togethers that are little more than another forum for issuing orders. The best companies listen to their customers about their needs, and the kudos and/or criticisms they have about the company and/or its people.

Does your company encourage you to work with fellow employees or leaders as a team? Do team members build on each other's strengths? Or is your company more about everyone working alone at his or her own speed and with his or her own approach? *Long-term success demands a focus on the same long-range goals, as opposed to various teams or groups working in different directions.*

Does your company have a version of a Meeting in a Box? Do meetings at your company have substance? Are they considered an important way to communicate what's happening and reinforce company values and goals? Or are they considered more of a nuisance and a hassle that everyone tries to avoid? *If the latter is the standard at your company, it's time to reassess and think through the content of those meetings. Meetings should be a regular important form of interactive communication and direction—an idea exchange, too. After all, it's about maintaining focus on the tasks at hand, capitalizing on team member strengths, and everyone working toward the same long-range goals.*

CHAPTER 7

The Customer's Success Is Your Success

Happier employees translate into happier customers.

—Diane K. Adams

Your customer's experience translates into your success or failure. When your customers succeed, so do you financially. That's the reality behind those oft-tired words at many companies, "The customer comes first."

The Value of Customer Experience

Many of us—myself included—like to shop, whether for business or pleasure, at companies where the employees know and welcome you. They pay attention to your personal needs and work hard to make the experience memorable.

Personal Service

Fab'rik is one of my favorite boutiques. It's actually an Atlanta-based franchise with stores throughout the Southeast and spreading across the country. Whenever I visit one of their stores, wherever it is, it's always with the same great results. When you walk in the door, immediately a smiling clerk is there to greet you. Even if you've never been in the store before, the clerk will spend a few minutes to get to know you and your style. Then she'll make the experience fun by pulling out clothes and accessories that typically you wouldn't think you would wear, but that you absolutely love and that look great on you.

Fab'rik's people make the experience fun and worthwhile from the moment you walk in the door. Result: you buy what you totally didn't plan on, and the company makes more money in the process. Win-win on all accounts.

Evereve is another chain of boutiques that's become a huge success, in part thanks to its customer care and service attitude. From one boutique in Edina, Minnesota, it's grown in just ten years to more than 50 stores coast to coast. That growth has happened through a recession, too.

Not New

No matter where or what your business may be, this kind of customer service revolving around personal service isn't a new concept. Plenty of mom and pop businesses have successfully practiced it for years.

Companies of all sizes, too, spend billions of dollars every year to buy technologies that promise better customer service.

No Excuses

What happens regularly, though, is that many of those same companies think technology is enough to create the great customer experience. It's not. Many companies also claim the cost of training and the effort involved is too high.

Whatever size your company may be—from one employee to one thousand and up—you can't afford not to train your employees and to insist on their delivering top customer service.

Overwhelmingly, (almost seven out of ten) customers say one bad experience is all it takes to prompt them to stop doing business with a company, according to a recent Harris/Avaya study. "Ask the customer to jump too many hurdles to get the service they desire, and a company is more likely to send them running in another direction," the study points out.[1]

For those companies that truly live the words "the customer comes first," and practice genuine exceptional customer service, it's a different story. And it's another essential value for a culture that sustains growth and success.

Eight out of ten respondents in the study also agree that other important aspects of the customer experience include

- an agent's knowledge of a product or service and
- a friendly and engaging agent.

One and Done

Here's an easy-to-relate-to example of poor customer service and what it can do to a business. Many of you have probably had a similar experience.

Recently I was in New York, and after a long day of meetings, was looking forward to a relaxing meal with my team. We chose a well-respected Italian restaurant. Unfortunately, however, the service was so poor that by the time the meal was over, my team was more anxious and exhausted than recharged.

The quality of the food may have been good, but it was overshadowed by the poor customer experience. It is likely none of us will eat there again.

Make It Extraordinary

When customer service is concerned, the goal of any business should be to make every experience exceptional for every customer. To do that means the following:

- **Exceed expectations.** Always do more and go beyond what the customer expects.
- **Make the experience personal.** Do your homework and know your customer.
- **Deliver within the expected time frame.** Better still, deliver the good or service ahead of schedule. That makes the experience memorable, and that in turn drives repeat business.
- **Expect to make exceptions to rules.** There always are exceptions to rules when the customer is concerned.

This kind of memorable customer service becomes the natural outgrowth of a company with an exceptional, values-based culture.

The Standard of Customer Service

Since its early days more than 100 years ago, retailing giant Nordstrom has been known for its impeccable customer service. It's a mega-chain, yet the personalized customer service feels more like that of a tiny boutique (think Fab'rik, above). The company's employee handbook lays out the "Nordstrom Rules":

"Rule #1: Use good judgment in all situations. There will be no additional rules."

The customer experience isn't just rhetoric at Nordstrom. For example, the retailer accepts any return for any reason, no questions asked. Of course, there's the shopper who buys the outfit on Friday, wears it over the weekend, and returns it on Monday. I always joke with Nordstrom salespeople about that because they know the buy/return scam happens.

But long ago, Nordstrom decided to focus on service, and not the occasional customer who abuses it. Nordstrom assumes correctly that most people don't buy something to wear it and return it. The net message instead is that, because of the chain's exceptional customer service, sales will go up. They have, too, along with company growth and expansion. Nordstrom earnings continue to exceed expectations.[2]

Catering to Your Customers

The 42nd Street Oyster Bar is my No. 1 food spot at Raleigh-Durham (North Carolina) International Airport. It's not strictly the food that draws me there, either. It's the personalized customer care—one server in particular—that brings me back regularly (With my Qlik job, I'm a regular flyer.) The server knows me, knows what I always order, and that I only have five to ten minutes to grab what I need before getting on the plane.

Know Your Customers. One early morning en route somewhere, I stopped at the Oyster Bar, picked up my meal, and headed down the concourse to catch my plane. I then realized that this server was running down the concourse after me. I stopped, and when he caught up, he explained that he knew I always ordered unsweetened tea, but that The Oyster Bar was out that day. He had gone to a neighboring restaurant and bought the tea for me so that I could have it with my meal.

Do the Unexpected. Can you imagine? It's not that I'm a big spender or tipper. All I buy is a $12 salad with a 20 percent tip. The server went to those lengths strictly for customer service. Not only is the service exceptional but it's also personal. And, as a result I'll never go to another restaurant at the airport, even if that server isn't there.

The Right Timing. I am just as devoted to my hairdresser, too—Bashir, in Raleigh. Again, it's about exceptional personal service. He knows I have an unusual and tight schedule. He always accommodates it. It's the same not only for me but also for members of my family, and others whom I have referred to his salon. He'll open the salon early or keep it open late, whatever meets his customers' needs.

Exceed Expectations. That's not the end, either. If it's early morning, he'll always have breakfast for his client. Dinner, too, if it's late. Yet his fees are in line with other salons. Again, he simply provides exceptional and personal customer service. Why then would anyone go anywhere else! His customers' experience is his success. That experience in turn develops repeat business.

More Top Service

Too many companies obsess over strategy when what they really should care about is creating and ingraining a culture that creates positive experiences for their customers.

René Carayol is a professor at the Cass Business School. In a podcast for the *Harvard Business Review*'s IdeaCast, he recounts a story that reminds us that customer experience is everything.[3]

Carayol prefaces the story by saying, "In the world I live in today, I feel very strongly that culture is more powerful than strategy.... When I say culture, I mean the way we get things done around here."

He goes on to recount a recent trip to the Beverly Wilshire Hotel in Los Angeles. It began with the desk clerk greeting him, "Welcome back to the Beverly Wilshire Hotel, Mr. Carayol."

"Well," says Carayol, "it stunned me because I've never stayed at the Beverly Wilshire Hotel."

Checking her computer, the clerk then politely pointed out the date of his last visit: "June, 1988. You were with a group of 12 from Marks and Spencer."

"Now that just knocked me out," says Carayol. "That's what I call service." Carayol then explained that he looked so pleased, the manager upgraded him to a suite. Now even more pleased, Carayol headed upstairs to take a quick shower. Before the shower, though, he tweeted about the hotel's great customer service.

By the time he got out of the shower, there was a tweet back from the general manager of the hotel thanking him for his comments and adding, "I'll come and find you and thank you in person."

That, says Carayol, is an organization that's agile and truly customer-centric. The service didn't stop there. Later, the hotel's manager sent him a bottle of high-end champagne, again thanking him for his tweet.

That's culture, says Carayol.

Carayol's epilogue to his story is a stark contrast to this best-culture experience. Back in London, he received a tweet from a woman who traveled on business to London every week for six years, and stayed at the same hotel. "I get a slightly different experience," she tweeted. "They ask me every Monday, 'Have you stayed with us before?'"

Expect and Plan for Exceptions to Rules

True customer service—not even the *exceptional* kind—means businesses must expect and plan for exceptions. No matter how big or small a company may be, there are always genuine exceptions to the rules. Businesses must plan for them and train their employees to expect them and in how to handle them.

Unfortunately, too often that's not the case. In the most extreme circumstances, that no-exceptions attitude can even have the potential for physically disastrous results.

Health and Well-Being. My parents are both in their 70s. They live in a single-family home and usually are self-sufficient. My dad, though, recently had back surgery. When we brought him home from the hospital, he was well enough not to require full-time hospitalization, but still needed regular visits from nurses and physical therapists.

When we got home, my mom discovered their cable service was out. That meant the telephone service was out, too. So, without a LAN line, my mother was worried, especially because of my father's health condition. She contacted her cable provider, Time Warner, explained the situation, and asked if they could get someone out "right away." The situation, she said, was an emergency because of my father's health.

No Exceptions! "Right away" and "emergency" for Time Warner in Raleigh-Durham—at least the employees my mother talked to—apparently isn't too fast. They adamantly told her the soonest they could get a technician to their home was one week. There were "NO exceptions."

My parents don't live in a distant rural area. They live in the middle of a major metropolitan area. Yet this major cable provider refused to provide two customers—one just released from the hospital following a major surgery—the assistance they needed to have a link to the outside world—either Internet or telephone.

That's not acceptable when it comes to customer service. There must be exceptions to rules.

Thankfully, there were no sudden medical emergencies during that week, and we were able to get my mother a temporary cell phone. But what if my parents hadn't had family nearby or the financial wherewithal to handle a potential crisis?

Whether your business has competition or not, that kind of lack of customer care does not foster long-term success. Adding to the insult of refusing to expedite my parents' request for help, Time Warner offered no extra service or cost break, which could have turned the situation more positive.

Across the Board

Poor customer service has no place in any business or industry. Instead, if a company provides great goods or services, with personalized and exceptional service, then customers will come back again and again through good and bad economic times.

With any customer and any business, ask yourself, what can you do to make that person's or that company's experience exceptional?

Take the time to know your customers, too. Relationships develop repeat business. If yours is a business-to-business transaction, do your homework to find out more about the company and its needs. Ask yourself what you and your employees can do that will exceed the customer's expectations. How can you accommodate the customer's time frame and make the experience memorable in a positive way?

Successful companies nurture a culture that promotes this kind of customer service and in turn helps build repeat business and develop long-term growth.

Above and Beyond

Lots of people scoffed at Richard Branson—his board of directors included—when he founded Virgin Atlantic Airways in 1984. The idea of a successful airline with all the perks seemed too simple and too out of reach.

Simple Concept. But Branson figured if he could establish the right culture, attract the right clientele, and provide impeccable service, his airline could succeed. From a start with one leased jumbo jet on one route, today it has a fleet that includes 39 aircraft that fly short and long hauls worldwide.[4]

No Slip-Ups. Branson remains a firm believer in providing the ultimate in customer service. One of Branson's businesses over the years was a condom manufacturing plant. (This is not a joke!)

A pregnant and dissatisfied customer sent him a nasty note about the failure of his product. Unfazed, Branson called the woman to apologize. The customer obviously was impressed by his customer concerns/service. A short time later, after her baby was born, she asked Branson to be the godfather.

Positive Returns

Kimpton is a San Francisco-based chain of more than 60 boutique hotels in 28 cities across the country that's all about creating an exceptional customer experience. I've stayed at Kimptons from New York to Chicago, Denver, and points west because no matter where I am, the service always is impeccable, the people friendly, and the accommodations pristine and spacious.

The customer's needs really do come first. That includes tastefully decorated rooms with plenty of light, storage space, and connections for electronics, as well as access to whatever I need. All those little things do matter.

And, I'll always go back to a Kimpton.

Happy (Profitable) Endings

One of the most famous restaurants in the Triangle region of North Carolina is Angus Barn. It's a steakhouse that's been known for its food and kitsch for decades. It's also regularly recognized for its quality and customer service. The latter even impresses me.

My daughter Kristen and her husband, Adam, held their wedding reception there several years ago in a pavilion by the lake behind the restaurant.

On their first wedding anniversary, the happy couple went back to Angus Barn for dinner. Afterward, they asked their server if it would be OK if they went out to the darkened pavilion to reminisce. The server responded, "We'll do one better than that. We'll open the pavilion and turn on the lights so you can have your 'first dance' again."

The Angus Barn has made its reputation by creating special moments like that, and as Kristen's experience demonstrates, continues to do so.

At Kristen and Adam's wedding reception, there were more than 250 people, yet the restaurant was attentive to everyone. I remember one guest who was allergic to seafood and had to send her meal back. Not only did they bring her another main course but they also changed out a side dish because the other one had been cooked in oil that had touched seafood. That's paying attention to the smallest detail to make sure a customer's experience is successful.

That kind of attention to detail is not by accident either. Angus Barn's owners work hard to provide extensive training to their team members. The customer's success is the restaurant's success. This business has been around for more than five decades, and continues to be in the Top 10 in its area, recognized for its customer service and food.[5]

Not Even Close

No matter where I am in the country, Uber, the independent car service, is always a great transportation option. They've always delivered on fair pricing and fast, dependable service.

Then came yet another business trip to New York City last year. I looked to Uber, assuming it would deliver the service I had come to expect. Unfortunately, it did not. One car that I called never showed up. Another did, but only after close to a half hour wait.

When a company—in this case, Uber—doesn't deliver on the promise of good service, its customers—myself included—go elsewhere.

Cementing the Relationship

Customer service and success is important in any business. After all, return customers are essential for long-term success.

Make It Right

While I was at Cisco, every Monday morning then-CEO John Chambers sent out voice mails to senior leaders highlighting which customers, if any, were experiencing challenges.

The voice mail also provided specific directions on how to support the customers and ensure their success. John knew that if his customers succeeded, Cisco would, too.

Personal Experiences

John knew the importance of developing long-term relationships with customers and with his employees, too. After all, statistics show that gaining a new customer—just as hiring a new employee—can cost well more than retaining a current one. With customers, the cost of developing a new one can range from 3 to 4, to up to 10 to 12 times that of retaining an old one.

John also took the time to prep for any meeting with a customer or other external engagement. Beforehand, he would pull together people with expertise on the topic and/or who knew the individual/individuals involved. His goal: to succinctly address the basics of what was happening; why it was happening; who was involved; and any associated pertinent relationships and points of view.

Similarly, he expected his teams to be thoroughly versed and well prepared for any meeting, too, so that he could quickly be briefed on what he needed to know.

Customer Satisfaction Surveys

A popular way in which many companies think they're creating a culture focused on customer success is by purchasing expensive customer satisfaction surveys. In concept, it's a good idea. Again, however, like company culture itself, execution falls short too often.

The reasons for these disappointing results are varied. Companies buy survey templates that may not be customized to their specific business or needs, and therefore don't reflect reality. Companies may commission others to do the surveys, and then fail to follow up on the results. Companies also may not take customer feedback seriously. Or companies may simply not pay attention to the details and the training that customer service requires.

More Than a Survey

Still another reason why satisfaction surveys come up short is that businesses think a survey is all it takes to bolster customer service.

As you've seen in the examples above, real and true customer service is about much more than administering a survey and collecting the data. It's about putting the customer first, providing personalized service and extraordinary and exceptional customer experiences, and making exceptions to satisfy a customer's needs.

Get the Real Story

Keep in mind, too, that asking your customers to rate their experiences with your company doesn't tell the entire story.

If you don't ask why, if you don't ask about the experience and the qualitative deal, too, you can't really understand what part of the customer experience needs to be addressed. For example, if someone had a bad experience, it could be the result of one person's actions rather than that the company isn't responsive or a problem with a process exists. You can't know that unless your customer satisfaction surveys ask the right questions that direct customers to provide the details.

I remember a situation at a Wisconsin-based company in which its initial customer feedback surveys had great questions, but they didn't go into enough detail to pinpoint the problem areas. Consequently, the end results were less than satisfactory.

However, once the survey was expanded to include greater detail, the company was able to identify the problems and make changes that led to positive results.

The Details

A customer satisfaction survey doesn't have to be formal or cost lots of money. It can be a simple phone call, email, or note to a customer to ask a few questions:

- How was your experience?
- What did we do right?
- What did we do wrong?
- (If we did something wrong...) How can we make it right?
- How can we make it better than "right"?
- How can we do better next time?

The Follow-Up. Most importantly, though, is the follow-up. If a customer had a poor experience or needs something additional, you must do the follow-up. Make sure that the customer's experience, instead of being negative, becomes positive—make it better than right.

One Customer at a Time. At Allscripts, we worked hard to create a culture focused on customer success.

One of the unusual approaches to customer satisfaction surveys involved 500 employees in a room at one time. We gave each employee a different customer's phone number, and then gave them all 15 minutes to call that customer.

Employees in turn individually called the customers, identified themselves and their title at Allscripts, and then asked about their experiences with the company. Questions included the following:

- What is it we do that you like and that is working?
- What don't you like or what isn't working?
- Is there anything else we can do for you?

If follow-up was involved, the company made sure it happened. Thanks to this exercise, in a very short amount of time we were able to connect with our customers, while cementing with our employees the importance of always thinking about the customer experience. The goal that we achieved was satisfied and successful customers as well as educated and caring employees.

Share the Results

Companies should openly share satisfaction survey results with their employees, too. That's an essential part of open communications and collaboration. After all, if a company AND its employees know what they're doing right and wrong, they're better positioned to improve their actions and relationships with customers.

A best practice at Qlik is to share quarterly our customer satisfaction numbers and comments across the entire company.

What's in a Name?

No matter the size of your company, you may want to think beyond naming your division, or even the title of the individual charged with focusing on customer success, simply "customer service."

Just as human resources is much more than that, and has morphed into culture and talent at successful companies, so should the moniker customer service.

For example, consider names like customer advocacy or customer success. Both names reinforce a culture that's proactive about taking care of its customers and creating exceptional experiences for them.

Culture Check/Customer Service

What's the bottom line when it comes to customer service at your company? Does your company really care about taking care of its customers, about meeting the needs of its customers, and about solving customer challenges, issues, and complaints? That's a tall order in any business. But that's also the key to real and true customer satisfaction, loyalty, and repeat business no matter the external economics. Long-term success is not about selling the most product or services. It's about satisfying customers and potential customers first. Sales become the natural outgrowth of customer service.

What does your company do to make a customer's or a potential customer's experience exceptional? Get to know your customers and develop relationships. Don't just meet a customer's needs. Exceed them. Make the experience memorable in a positive way.

Does your company have customer satisfaction surveys? If so, what, if anything, does your company do with the results? Are they long and involved, or short and sweet? Many companies have surveys, but they may not ask the right questions that will allow a company to fully identify its problems. The right kind of customer satisfaction survey—one that's short and to the point (what's right; what's wrong)—can be a valuable learning tool. And, they're the best way to get a real picture of team performance.

Does your company have formal follow-up procedures for customer kudos and complaints? This is an opportunity to develop those all-important customer relationships that can and do help sustain a company through good and bad economic times.

CHAPTER 8

Paying It Forward: Giveback and Social Responsibility

There's no greater reward personally and professionally than making a difference for others.

—*Diane K. Adams*

Strata Decisions, a small Chicago-based technology company, gives all of its 100 employees one day off a year to volunteer or give back to the community. The company calls that paid time off "Mensch Day." It's a popular success internally, and externally in the community. Many employees opt to volunteer on their own time, too. Inside the company's headquarters, walls are adorned with pictures of smiling employees engaged in various volunteer activities, from cross-country skiing with the disabled to serving dinners to the homeless, reading to kids, and more.

Technology giant HP gives each of its employees four hours per month on company time to volunteer or give back. Last year alone, its 40,000-plus employees worldwide contributed more than 1.6 million volunteer hours to thousands of activities—ranging from individual one-on-one assistance and guidance to team construction projects. Volunteers helped build a playground in Chicago, they sponsor a school for migrants in Beijing, China, they provide pro bono direction and advice to a major food bank, and more.[1]

High Value—Monetarily and More

These two companies in their own way recognize the importance and value of giving back. In 1947, Dave Packard, cofounder of Hewlett-Packard, famously said, "The betterment of society is not a job to be left to a few. It's a responsibility to be shared by all." That ethos is reflected in HP's gold standard volunteer policy today.[2]

Help for Veterans

Today's new face of giving back extends to helping returning military veterans find jobs, too. In 2011, a coalition of 11 companies formed the "100,000 Jobs Mission" (www.veteranjobsmission.com), which is committed to doing whatever is necessary—including targeted recruitment and training—to hire 100,000 military veterans by 2020. As of year-end 2014, the coalition had grown to more than 190 companies, representing nearly every industry, and has hired more than 217,000 veterans. The coalition's founding member companies include AT&T, Broadridge Financial Solutions, Inc., Cisco Systems Inc., Cushman & Wakefield Inc., EMC Corporation, Iron Mountain Incorporated, JPMorgan Chase & Co., Modis, NCR Corporation, Universal Health Services, Inc., and Verizon Communications Inc.

Many of those companies, including Cisco, also have joined forces with other public and private initiatives to further ensure the hiring of veterans. Cisco's John Chambers blogged last year: "We must provide the training, certifications, and jobs that our veterans have earned and deserve."[3]

Why Bother?

Giveback is about social responsibility. But it's also an essential ingredient for long-term company success.

When companies and their employees pay attention and give back to their communities, they grow their customer base and their bottom lines. They nurture happier and more engaged employees, and develop relationships with their customers and community that translate into dollars and cents returns.

Volunteering is a huge recruiting tool, too, especially for young people who want any company they work for to have flexibility and social responsibility.

The Numbers Don't Lie

I asked Jack Welch, author and former CEO of General Electric, about his views on what makes a great leader and a great company. The more a company and its leaders give back, the more successful both are, he told me. That's because, if you and your company are involved in the community and in helping others, that nurtures loyalty on the part of customers and employees, and that loyalty will sustain a company during the toughest economic times.

The proof is in the numbers. Let's look at a few statistics from studies that examine the benefits of volunteering through an employer.

Less Attrition and Fewer Sick Days. Companies with employees who give back to the community have happier employees, and have lower attrition rates and better bottom lines in good times and bad. Attrition, after all, is costly. The tab to replace one lost employee can be up to three times that employee's annual salary, according to numbers from Gallup.

Unhappy employees—those who score low in "life satisfaction"—miss an average of 1.25 more work days a month than happy employees, according to results from a Gallup Healthways study. Life satisfaction is a widely accepted, commonly tested metric associated with studies that examine workplace attitudes and efficiencies. In the Gallup study, those additional lost days of work translated into a decrease in productivity of 15 days a year.[4]

More Income. In looking at the value of positive intelligence, Jennifer George and Kenneth Bettenhausen studied service departments and found that employees who score high in life satisfaction are significantly more likely to receive high ratings from customers. Gallup research also found that retail stores that scored higher on employee life satisfaction generated $21 more in earnings per square foot of space than the other stores, adding $32 million in additional profits for the entire chain examined in the study.[5]

Positive Attitudes. People who volunteer through their employer have more positive attitudes toward that employer and their colleagues, too. That's the conclusion of a 2010 United Healthcare/Volunteer Match study. Study findings include the following:

- 81 percent of employees say volunteering with their work colleagues strengthens relationships.
- 76 percent feel better about their employer as a result of volunteer activities.
- 21 percent say they would not volunteer if it weren't for the opportunities and direction provided by their employer.[6]

The Millennial Connection. A corporate culture of giveback makes a big difference in hiring and retaining millennials. Seven in 10 favor companies that are committed to their communities, according to the eighth annual Deloitte Volunteer IMPACT Survey.

Millennials who frequently participate in their company's employee volunteer activities are

- twice as likely to rate their corporate culture as very positive (56 percent vs. 28 percent);
- more likely to feel very loyal toward their company (52 percent vs. 33 percent); and
- more likely to recommend their company to a friend (57 percent vs. 46 percent).[7]

Dollars and Cents of Volunteering

HP developed a metric to measure the value and impact of volunteering that accounts for both volunteer hours and pro bono professional services. Based on that measure, in 2012 alone HP's employees donated about 1.4 million hours, with a value of more than $85 million.[8]

That's no small change.

No Excuses

Despite these kinds of positive financials and feel-good results associated with social responsibility, giveback isn't the norm in big or small corporate America and beyond, however. Only one in four people who volunteer say it's through their place of work, and nearly six of ten say their employers don't even encourage volunteering, according to that United Healthcare/Volunteer Match survey.[9]

As with culture in general, many companies and their leaders simply think they can't afford the time or money to bother with worrying about social responsibility.

Any company, though, can and must afford to give back in some way. If you still think you can't start small, think again. Helping others can begin with one person, one cause, and one hour at a time.

The Multiplier Effect

But be forewarned. Big or small, doing good for others is contagious.

I call this the multiplier effect. In and out of the workplace, when people volunteer, wherever they volunteer, what happens will surprise you. So will the resulting increase in enthusiasm (and in production) among your employees.

At Allscripts

While I was at Allscripts, the company gave millions of dollars in donated time and money annually. That happened because, rather than spend money on fancy "team-building" exercises, Allscripts opted to encourage its people to live its strong culture of social responsibility.

All 500 leaders in the company, along with their teams, were required twice a year to participate in givebacks. That's two days annually at company expense—1,000 givebacks a year for whatever cause or the charitable institution or event was chosen by each of the teams.

For example, I remember visiting an autism center for children in India that was set up, supported, and partially funded by Allscripts' staff there. Some other examples of Allscripts' giveback range from collecting thousands of pounds of food for food banks in various cities to donating hundreds of pints of blood to the Red Cross, supporting the Juvenile Diabetes Research Foundation (JDRF), building houses for Habitat for Humanity, and raising money for disaster relief in Manila, the Philippines, and Haiti.

Cisco Rallies behind JDRF

When my daughter Danielle was diagnosed with type I diabetes, she was 4, and I still worked at Cisco. Scott Brown, then a vice president of worldwide operations and support who worked out of the company's Research Triangle Park (North Carolina) office, and his executive assistant, Lori Volpi, decided to rally team members to join the JDRF Walk to Cure Diabetes. Danielle's diagnosis spotlighted others with diabetes in the community, too.

Then came the multiplier effect. More and more people joined the annual walk. Years later, the event continues today. People in Cisco's North Carolina offices literally have raised hundreds of thousands of dollars for JDRF. They have fun doing it, too. Employees' kids participate in T-shirt design contests, executives hold fundraising car washes and pancake breakfasts, and teams hold bake sales.

I remember another event at which a group of Cisco employees got together as a band; they rented out a venue and charged a cover to guests to raise money for JDRF. At the time, Danielle wasn't a teenager yet, but there she was on stage singing with them the Iggy Pop song "Keep on Believing"!

Developing the Giveback Mentality

You and your company can do this, too. You don't have to be a Fortune 500 company. But you do have to make the conscious effort to give back, whatever the cause or the crusade.

Remember Quicken Loans, the company with the award-winning culture I introduced you to in chapter 3? Its CEO sends all of his thousands of employees personally signed birthday cards.

The company has played a major role in the revitalization of its hometown of Detroit. It's donated millions of dollars to the community, and its team members have volunteered tens of thousands of hours at nonprofit organizations there.

Said Quicken CEO Bill Emerson in 2014, "Of everything we accomplished last year, what makes me the most proud is that our team still took time to lend a hand to those in need in the communities where we live, work and play. It is that passion for doing the right thing and caring about others that lays the groundwork for our success."[10]

Effective Giveback Programs

What creates this kind of enthusiasm, camaraderie, and passion for a cause? It starts with a company's high values and the right approach to giving back.

Nearly every successful employee volunteer program—EVP in the jargon—includes variations on the same themes and processes. So, whatever approach to giveback you, your company, or your employees choose, keep in mind the following elements that can contribute to its chances for success.

Company-Sponsored Causes

Company-sponsored causes—Quicken and Detroit, for example—have a greater chance of ongoing success in terms of donating dollars and time because the sponsorship generally means greater impact.

Often the cause will be one favored by the company's owner or chosen by the C-suite. Another best practice gives employees, not the bosses, the voice and the choice of the specific cause or causes to support. One of the advantages of this approach is that with more individual personal commitment, the impact can be greater.

And sometimes, the approach to giveback is a combination of both.

Time to Volunteer

Successful companies know the importance of giving all their employees time off for the purpose of giveback.

There's no better time than now to start your giveback and to accept the social responsibility that becomes a part of success. All of your employees should receive at minimum at least one day a year, *in addition to* vacation time, to volunteer and give back to the community.

If your company is small and/or just starting out, even if all you can do at first is an hour off here or there for an employee, or a small donation of products or services, it's a start. These actions become the foundation for a commitment to social responsibility and should be the beginning of regular and growing volunteerism.

Team-Building Efforts

Giveback is a powerful team-building exercise. It's the same kind of team-building that companies spend lots of money and time trying to teach their employees—often unsuccessfully.

But with giveback, the benefits are greater and more far reaching than those often inane, off-site, supposedly team-building events. When people volunteer and help others, they're energized and engaged. They gain a sense of purpose, learn to work together, and make a difference while doing it. Even when things are tough financially, if people give back to others, they hold onto the fact they are part of a winning team that's making a difference. What's happening around them—tough economic conditions, for example—doesn't matter.

So, instead of expending the effort to force your employees as a team to drive go-karts, hike, crawl around in the mud, or do some other exotic and often expensive team-building exercise, consider a team giveback instead. The benefits to you and your company and team will be much bigger, and the success much greater and more widespread.

Remember the Deloitte survey of millennials mentioned earlier? Not only does volunteering have a positive effect on millennial attitudes toward their employers, but when it comes to career progression, those who volunteer are nearly twice as likely to be very satisfied with the development of their career and with their employer.

"At a time when one-third of millennial employees are considering other career options, these findings may offer new insights about a powerful way to engage workers among this age group," Deloitte wrote in the report.[11]

Recognition and Praise

As important as the volunteering is, so is how you, your executive team, and your company showcase, praise, and recognize what people do to give back. This action on your part is about letting others know that the culture at your business supports community caring.

Strata Decisions provides its employees wall space to post volunteer opportunities, and then showcases photos of its employees as they volunteer. There's also a bulletin board in their break room for posting volunteer opportunities.

Larger companies with their own Intranets, like Cisco and Allscripts, showcase giveback there, too, so that everyone knows what's being done. Intranets also provide an outlet for posting volunteer opportunities as well as bragging about accomplishments.

We're all little kids at heart and enjoy showing off what we do, especially when it truly makes a difference.

Make It Fun

Just like a company's culture, volunteering can be fulfilling and fun. Your company can help make it that way if the following is true:

- **It's an easy extension of a job.** That means someone doesn't have to beg for the time off or lose pay because he or she volunteers for or supports a cause, even in his or her off-hours. Volunteering must not create hassles at work.
- **The cause or volunteer work is a personal or professional commitment.** It could be a cause chosen by an employee or a team. Perhaps a

fellow employee, family, or friends have suffered a loss, or there's a need. Together, a team rallies to help.

- **It's not approached as a job.** Instead, it involves doing something that helps others.

How to Find Your Cause

You can create a commitment to giveback at your company, too. Find the right cause and get started today.

BENEFITS OF VOLUNTEERING

The nonprofit Points of Light Foundation offers its take on the value of volunteering, saying that it

- *boosts employee morale, teambuilding, loyalty, productivity, motivation, and reduces absenteeism;*
- *attracts new hires, especially millennials;*
- *reaches more clients and increases sales, and therefore has a positive impact on profitability;*
- *builds stronger communities by addressing social issues;*
- *illustrates organizational values in action; and*
- *demonstrates corporate support for activities that allow employees to spend quality time with their families.*

Source: PointsofLight.org[12]

What Works with Your Business?

Identifying how you can give back doesn't have to be difficult. Consider, for example, what are one or two primary causes that may fit with the mission statement of your company or a personal mission? Think about your business or industry, too. What is your area of expertise? How do your products or services help others? Is there a natural fit in terms of donating those products or performing various services?

If you're a technology company, you might consider investing in education. Many companies donate products or create programs that help in the field of education because technology is a key enabler. Giveback provided by health-care companies often involves health care, a primary area of company expertise. Construction or engineering companies often work with nonprofits like Habitat for Humanity, which builds homes for those who need them.

Employee Choices

Ask employees what matters to them. After all, they're the ones who will come together and rally in support of a cause.

Givebacks don't have to be global in scope or even part of big organizations. They can be local or even personal. Picking up trash on the street can make a big difference for your community. So does building a desperately needed playground at a nearby school, or tutoring a child who needs help.

You as a person or as a member of a team that's part of a company must decide what's important. If it's a companywide cause, perhaps it involves helping a fellow employee who has been diagnosed with breast cancer, or the owner of a favorite meeting spot who suffers from a debilitating disease. The right cause, therefore, might be to raise money for that individual or an organization that supports research and treatment of that disease.

Is there a local race or event for which you can sponsor a team or your team can become a participant? Or, think about other ways you can make a difference in the life of that person. Does he or she or do his or her family members need physical assistance? Maybe the right giveback cause for you and/or your company is to provide transportation to those who don't have it.

When there's commitment on the part of your company, your giveback is limited only by your imagination and the amount of time you can provide.

Getting Started

If you're getting started organizing a giveback for your company, familiarity and association can often be a participation motivator in the beginning. But, as I mentioned earlier, volunteering is contagious.

Once one person does it, there is a multiplier effect. You influence others to give back, too, and they in turn influence still others.

More Information

Making the job of giveback even easier, there are a number of government, nonprofit, and other organizations that provide volunteering information and guidance, and even training.

Here are a few places to start.

- A Billion + Change Campaign (www.abillionpluschange.org): formed in 2008 as a campaign to leverage $1 billion in skilled volunteer and pro bono services from the corporate community; includes resources and information on pro bono services, setting up programs, and volunteering
- idealist (www.idealist.org): a nonprofit source of volunteer opportunities, events, and resources
- Points of Light Foundation (www.pointsoflight.org): created as an independent, nonpartisan, nonprofit organization to encourage and empower the spirit of service
- Volunteer Match (www.volunteermatch.org): a national nonprofit that connects volunteers with opportunities and causes

Culture Check/Giveback

Giveback is a social responsibility that long-term successful companies of all sizes take very seriously. The best companies make it an integral part of their culture.

What's your company's attitude toward giving back to others? Does the company embrace it and give its leaders and employees paid time off to volunteer? Does the company reward or recognize its employees who give back?

Or does the company say it's great to volunteer as long as it's on your own time? Or, is yours a company with leaders who say they're too busy or the company can't afford to bother with giving back? Don't let your company make excuses for not being socially responsible, for not giving back to the community, and for not embracing employees who like to volunteer.

What makes a giveback successful? Does it have full company support? Are there rewards and/or recognition for social responsibility? If so, what? If not, what can you do to positively impact giveback programs at your company?

If your company has a giveback program, is it a cause chosen by employees or dictated by leaders? Often the most successful causes are those selected by consensus that in some way relate to a company's fabric or its industry.

How might your company further encourage a giveback culture among its team members? Think about unique and unusual ways in which you can encourage that. At Qlik, for example, we pay team members for new-employee referrals. The payment is in the form of cash as well as a contribution to the nonprofit of their choice. What a great way for the company to emphasize its giveback culture!

CHAPTER 9

Learning Is Your Edge: Invest in Your People

People join a company for the opportunity. They stay for the investment.

—*Diane K. Adams*

Money alone isn't enough to keep employees.

People may join your company for the cash, but they stay when they're engaged, when they're challenged, and when you invest in them. Successful companies care enough about their teams to provide the learning, education, and encouragement necessary to continually grow. Their companies grow, too.

A number of years ago when my kids were still small, I had a successful consulting business. As my own boss, I liked the independence and freedom, and the challenges of working with various companies. Then Cisco and John Chambers came calling.

What lured me away from my own business wasn't the money. It was the challenge and potential learning experience of building and scaling a company's culture at one of the world's fastest growing companies at the time.

The Value of Talent

The best companies and their leaders recognize that talent is the edge. Therefore, value your people and invest in them.

Does your company do that? Or, instead, does its leadership see only the dollars and cents involved, treat employees as expendable commodities, and refuse to make the conscious commitment to provide continuing education and new skills?

One of those companies that does recognize what its people bring to the table is SEPI Engineering. To that end, CEO Sepi Saidi encourages her teams to learn and grow professionally and personally. She's intentional about creating a company and in turn careers that enable her people to reach their potential. That's an essential ingredient in a long-term successful company.

In 13 years, Sepi has grown her private engineering firm from a start-up in a back room in her home to three offices across North Carolina and more than $20 million in revenues. Much of that growth came during the last major recession.

Profits at Sepi's company continue to grow today, in part because her company's culture is built around empowering her teams to work together with innovation and success top of mind.

The Value of Commitment

The company advertises, "We are truly committed to focusing on the individual needs and contributions of every person who joins our team." Those aren't just words. They're the SEPI way of life. I'm a member of SEPI's outside board of directors, and I've watched them do just that for years.

Talk to SEPI employees and they'll tell you, Sepi just doesn't talk about learning, career growth, collaboration, and communications. Her teams live the values and learn from them every day. They're a "family" working together toward common goals. Team members solicit input from each other, they listen, they learn from each other, and they work together to develop solutions. The same thing happens whether it's a problem in the office or a project in the field. That's simply the way SEPI does business.

Says one SEPI manager, money is not everything.

Intentional and Personal

"A lot of what we focus on here is if someone needs training, we give it to them. If someone needs help with something, we help," says Marisa L. Mansfield, SEPI human resources manager. "We want you to succeed with the company."

At any company, that kind of attitude and approach reinforces to your teams and your customers that you care that your employees are at their best and that your company's work is at its best.

After all, in work and in life, it's the best team that wins, whether it's a team of Olympic athletes or software engineers, a football team or operators on an assembly line.

Cash or Not!

Investing in your employees and their education may sound like a call for major cash infusions. Who can afford this? Certainly not small businesses nor all but the biggest cash-rich companies.

Myth versus Reality

As with culture itself, though, investing in your employees and helping them learn and grow doesn't have to be overly difficult or expensive. Any costs on the front end, will pay back with dividends, too.

Encouraging your team members' curiosity doesn't carry a big price tag. Nor does helping them learn and grow in their careers. That can be a matter of promoting innovation, trust, on-the-job training, or mentoring. Mentoring, for example, is about caring and teaching your knowledge to others. The biggest expense is a company's willingness to commit to it.

Providing employees with opportunities for growth can be as easy as empowering and encouraging them to share knowledge with each other and work together to solve customer or product issues or problems, or giving them the chance to figure out a better way to achieve a goal—all within the stated values of the company. That's real engagement.

Even If It Costs...

Not doing the actions mentioned above, however, is an expensive mistake. Employees often end up disappointed, disillusioned, and disengaged. Some jump ship, while others languish in their jobs. Your productivity and profits may suffer as a result.

You simply can't afford not to invest in the growth and careers of your employees. Before you say, "no way," consider the cost if you don't. The average cost to replace an employee was more than $3,400, including recruiting, interviewing, hiring, training, and reduced productivity, according to numbers from the Society of Human Resource Executives.[1]

That's a lowball estimate, says Ross Blake, a retention expert, and the author of *10 Strategies to Develop an Effective Employee Retention Program.*

Ross' research should make you think again about NOT investing in your employees.

He estimates the cost to replace an entry-level employee at 30 percent to 50 percent of his or her annual salary. For a midlevel employee, it's 150 percent of annual salary, and up to 400 percent of annual salary for high-level, specialized employees.

In real numbers, to replace a $40,000/year supervisor would cost a company $50,000. If the company lost ten supervisors, that's $500,000 in bottom-line replacement costs. If that same company has a 10 percent profit margin, then it costs $5 million in revenues to replace these ten supervisors.[2]

Those are tough numbers. But it's an expense that in many cases can be avoided if a company cares about its employees and works to keep them engaged and learning, and growing. The company's success is the dividend that comes along with it!

How to Develop Your Talent

We develop talent in basically three ways:

- 10 percent through traditional classroom education
- 20 percent with exposure/mentoring
- 70 percent through experience

Therefore, a company that's committed to the learning and the growth of its employees should provide its team members with the tools to develop personally and professionally. That includes the following:

- **Career Opportunities**: Employees need to know they have a future and that you are willing to invest in that future in the form of education and training, and personal support and mentoring. In organizations with solid learning cultures, every employee has a personalized learning development plan.
- **Communications**: Two-way sharing of knowledge is an excellent learning tool. That means creating a collaborative workplace, as opposed to one that's strictly top-down command and control.
- **Compensation/Benefits**: Compensation/benefits don't have to be top tier, but they must be fair and equitable. Again, it's about a willingness to commit to and invest in your teams.

- **Recognition/Feedback:** Along with recognition comes powerful feedback, which in turn can provide a learning experience for everyone. In addition to quarterly reviews, the best leaders provide ongoing feedback as a natural element of their communications.
- **Senior Leadership:** Teams need leaders to set the example and to mentor others. Remember, culture, as in living a company's values, comes from the top.
- **Employee Morale:** Ongoing education and learning, along with competitive compensation and benefits—including perks—have an impact on morale and commitment to growth. Don't decide to slash benefits without regard for how that might sap team energy, commitment, and morale.

Beyond the Classroom

The bottom line is that helping your teams learn and grow goes well beyond hiring a teacher and bringing your employees together in a room.

Investing in the personal growth and development of your people—and helping ensure your company's success over the long term—should be a part of everyday work life, of how you do business, and of your company's culture.

Workable Approaches to Learning

Often organizations come up with creative solutions to train and educate employees and to incentivize learning.

Allscripts, for example, partnered with the US Department of Health and Human Services to develop a certification program for its software at community colleges across the country. Allscripts employees could attend and develop their expertise on the software. The classes also became a means of aggressively creating new talent for the company and the industry.

New Jersey-based Johnson & Johnson (NYSE: JNJ), the health-care products manufacturer, helps employees and leaders learn and grow through an elaborate two-way feedback program. Instead of a typical performance measurement tool—with many categories, ratings, and so on—employees rate their leaders' performance. Those results help identify areas and behaviors that need improvement. The feedback also serves as a tool to monitor whether behaviors are consistent with the company's values.

The company then quickly knows the type of training and education required to reinforce strengths and shore up weaknesses.

Leveraging Your Talent

In your company, whatever its size, team members can help each other learn and grow, whether in small groups or in all-hands meetings, via social media, or with the latest virtual technologies. That kind of communication and collaboration, as I've discussed throughout this book, is an essential ingredient at successful companies.

So is engaging your people who have expertise in one area to teach other team members. That's yet another reason to hire and put together teams whose members have varied expertise. That expertise may be the result of past experience or come from the off-site training of one team member, who in turn then trains others. The latter, for example, happens all the time with new technologies.

Be careful, though. Just because one team member knows how to do something, doesn't mean the rest of the team "will figure it out" on their own. Essential to leveraging talent is making sure the learning and training is intentional. You must make the time for your people to have the opportunity to learn, grow, and contribute.

Meeting Is Learning

Simply getting together and interacting can be a learning experience. At Qlik, we understand that. Once a year the company holds an annual summit for all its employees. Last year, the summit was in Cancun, and the company paid for everyone to travel there.

This is a big expense, but an important one because, as a result, every employee has the opportunity to interact with each other, to fully understand what's happening at the company, and to learn about our current goals. Everyone recognizes, too, that he or she is a valued member of the team, and this experience conveys to everyone that Qlik is willing to invest in the development of its employees.

Bringing People Together

Realistically, every company can't afford the expense of packing up the team—whatever the size—and heading to an island getaway. But every company can operate with a culture that values its people, that promotes learning and education, broad participation and inclusion, and success.

None of that has to be costly. The practice has to do with getting people together to communicate, to learn, to motivate and teach each other, to develop relationships, and to recognize achievements.

Inexpensive Alternatives. A company could set the stage for learning via an occasional—maybe once a month or quarterly—pitch-in lunch or dinner. The company could pick up the tab for drinks or dessert. Breakfast or donuts and coffee for everyone works well, too. So does grabbing an occasional cup of coffee or meal one-on-one or in groups. That's in addition to using social media and the latest technologies to stay connected with your teams.

Whether you're the boss, a leader, or simply a team member, all those scenarios can be learning experiences and convey that you care and that the company cares. At these in-person meetings, share experiences, teach each other, celebrate successes, and talk about problems. Participants leave a bit wiser. They'll know their input matters, too, because it does at successful companies.

Lunch and Learn

One of my favorite ways to encourage learning is "lunch and learn." This practice can work at any size company. Gather the team together for lunch and bring in a speaker with a particular expertise that dovetails with your team's needs. I do this all the time with my team when we face a new challenge. In fact, one of the best learning experiences is to tap someone with a particular expertise in your company to do the teaching.

This is an inexpensive approach that transfers new knowledge, creates camaraderie and collaboration, and reinforces to your employees that you understand the issues they face and that you care.

When we hire someone new, we get the team together for lunch on the company's dime. We usually order in sandwiches, and sit and talk. It's a great way to make connections, nurture relationships, and share knowledge.

This kind of interaction should be a practice at your company, too, whether you are taking the time to get to know a new employee or a new customer or to learn something new.

This approach is also a great way to reinforce existing relationships. If you're the boss, take a person or a team to lunch. Your willingness to invest in a person conveys his or her value to the team.

A word of advice: if your reaction to the suggestion of going to lunch with your team or colleagues is, "why would I want to spend extra time with those people?" it's time to rethink your management style and/or your hiring practices.

Utilize Incentives

Though most people thirst for new knowledge, it's not always in the form of openly clamoring to learn and grow in our jobs. Sometimes we as leaders chalk up an employee's perceived lack of caring or unwillingness to learn something new to human nature.

Other times, it could be that the person has languished in his or her job or career as a result of boredom, what seems like a lack of caring about the job, or a previous lack of encouragement to develop skills and/or set stretch goals. Or, someone simply could be too busy in his or her job and not realize the importance of making the time to learn.

Whatever the reason or the roadblock, incentives can be the catalyst that triggers learning, personal and professional growth, and success.

Payback with Dividends

While I was at Allscripts, for example, leaders annually were required to complete a specific curriculum to strengthen their skill sets. To fast-track learning, the company offered free e-readers to leaders who completed the coursework in only 6 as opposed to 12 months. The promotion was a win-win-win for everyone. Leaders learned new skills more quickly and took home a Kindle, teams improved faster, and the company was the better for it.

Another great incentive: if you try "lunch and learns" with your team, offer a gift certificate to a local restaurant or the movies to the team or team member who applies the new skill or technology first or most effectively.

What about Employee Resistance?

In a perfect world, everyone wants to improve. We all love feedback— positive and negative—and aren't the slightest bit afraid of change. We can't wait to do things differently. After all, our goal is to become extraordinary in our lives and jobs as fast as possible.

Of course, we all know that's not what happens in life. Resentment of feedback and resistance to change are all too common aspects of the human psyche. They can be rampant in the workplace, especially at companies that haven't yet recognized the importance of positive values as a part of their culture.

Resentment manifests as workplace jealousies, backstabbing, negative energy, and more, especially when it's allowed. Remember, culture and the behaviors and attitudes that go with it, come from the top. It's the leadership that allows and/or overlooks those negative, pox-like actions and attitudes.

Sometimes who-finishes-first contests with prizes can be enough to effect the desired change. Other times, an employee must understand the serious consequences of refusing to change—job loss, for example. In that case, however, it may already be too late. An individual may be too entrenched in his or her unwillingness to learn something new. He or she then becomes the bad apple that threatens the team, making separation (firing) the only effective solution.

Separation, though, isn't always a quick fix. Remember the leader who at first wouldn't even hear what his employees had to say about his management style? He simply didn't want to change. But then, after thinking about it for a time, he changed his mind-set, sought out the criticism, and took it as what it was—a constructive way to learn to improve in his job. He became a much better leader for it.

Had it not been for his change of mind, the long-time leader would have been terminated. No company can afford the negativity and unrest that someone unwilling to change, learn, and grow can bring to an the entire team.

Stop First to Analyze the Weaknesses, Then Make Changes

That doesn't mean whenever an employee rebels, you should remove him or her. It's not that clear-cut. There's no one-size-fits-all solution.

If you find yourself in a similar situation, take the time to fully analyze the situation and circumstances, weigh the options, and above all, make sure you provide the individual with the opportunities and support he or she needs to change and grow. In the case of the manager above, I worked closely with him to help him learn what he needed to change.

The Importance of Change

What employers may overlook in their hiring, as well as in everyday operations, is that almost every employee brings something that matters to the table. His or her skills usually can make a difference given the opportunity to share that knowledge and work together as part of a team.

A technology company hadn't yet fully realized that. Its sales team attrition was a high 30 percent. A big part of the problem was that leaders had not invested in their team's growth and development, nor were they motivating and inspiring the team members. There was little recognition or reward for a job well done. And, there was the mistaken perception on the part of the team that management simply didn't care.

Education and Retention

Before it was too late, however, the company identified the problems and made the necessary changes. In just six months, attrition dropped by more than half.

How did that happen? The leadership invested in helping teams learn new skills, gave them challenging work, and began to reward and recognize team members for a job well done. All that is the norm in a values-based culture. But these basic actions had been overlooked in this case. Once the company started to pay attention to these basics, the organization had more satisfied employees, which in turn meant fewer employee defections and a reduction in the costs associated with new hires.

Putting Together Your Company's Learning Plan

As with most aspects of culture, creating the learning and personal growth plan that's right for your company depends on many things. No one size fits all here, either.

Essential aspects of any plan, though, are that it should be formal, involve specific and ongoing goals, provide for regular occurrences, and offer a formal assessment procedure.

At Allscripts, for example, during my tenure the company developed an extensive leadership review and succession-planning process. Every executive reviewed every director and his or her bosses with the goal of identifying those individuals with high potential who might be prepared to take on additional responsibilities and move up to various positions in the company. CEO Glen Tullman and I (as EVP Culture and Talent) thoroughly went over the reviews with leaders.

Allscripts further invested in its teams through an Accelerated Leadership Program for high-potential company directors and leaders at the University of North Carolina.

Lastly, the company incorporated specific leadership behaviors into its review of the performance of individuals. Behaviors that mattered included measuring client communications and collaboration. We were very prescriptive about our expectations in order to accelerate the strengthening of our leadership team. We expected leaders and up-and-coming leaders to integrate Allscripts' strong approach to two-way communications into everything they did. That meant that these leaders were expected to participate in ongoing learning and education, listening forums, lunch and learns, and so on.

This was a company that took the career growth of its teams very seriously.

Stop to Celebrate

Beyond information, direction, and advice, fun plays a role in workplace success, too. Few people day in and day out want to go into a business environment that's not upbeat. The right workplace demands a certain amount of celebration and fun, as in rewards, recognition, and camaraderie.

That doesn't mean all the bells, whistles, and banners that come with a party—though there's a place for that, too. Remember the Allscripts New Year's Eve celebration in February? Top of mind for Allscripts wasn't to party. Rather, it was to celebrate its employees, their accomplishments, and hard work.

Step Back, Praise, and Learn

Successful companies with engaged employees aren't afraid to stop and step back, even if briefly. They talk about, praise, and celebrate each other's accomplishments—personal and professional, a job or a project well done, and even customer accomplishments.

These same companies make it a priority to go back and review what's right and what's wrong with a project, situation, sale, accomplishment, or lack thereof. That kind of review becomes a major tool in growth and learning for all team members.

Unfortunately, that's not the norm at the vast majority of companies. Researchers at Aberdeen Group found that only 14 percent of companies empower their managers with the tools necessary to reward and recognize employees for their work.[3]

A Differentiator

Fun is serious. With the right leadership and processes ingrained in day-to-day business, employees actually enjoy coming to work, and work hard to grow and learn.

That's infinitely possible at successful companies. Time after time, year after year, employees at companies on the CNN/Fortune 100 Best Companies to Work For list mention that they enjoy their work and their workplace.

Think about what *you* can do to make *your* workplace fun, with the serious goal of personal and professional success in mind. How can you recognize and reward employees for a job well done? How can you leverage those successes into learning experiences for others? What will it take to positively reinforce learning and career growth?

The answers to those kinds of questions depend on your company, its culture, goals, and aspirations.

Great Approach

At Allscripts we had a fun way of recognizing employee contributions and reinforcing positive behaviors. The approach is easy to emulate at any company. Leaders regularly awarded Peer Recognition Certificates to employees for significant accomplishments throughout the year. The certificates came with Spot Awards—$50–$250 in gift cards. Those cards were customized to the recipient—perhaps an Italian restaurant for someone who liked Italian food, tickets to a musical for someone who enjoyed that kind of entertainment, or a movie for a film buff.

More importantly, the minimal-cost awards paid dividends because they involved people sharing with others, such as a friend, spouse, or significant other. Again, this practice demonstrated that our employer truly cared about us.

New Hire Orientation and Beyond

The right way to invest in your people starts from the beginning—with new hires. Tossing a new hire or any untrained employee into the mire and hoping he or she comes up breathing—the typical sink-or-swim approach—is not the fastest or the best approach to a successful culture. Laying a foundation for caring and ongoing learning and growth is.

Even if you've already done the hiring, or perhaps acquired another fully staffed company, it's not too late to establish a new foundation of values that can lead to greatness and extraordinary success.

Don't be afraid or hesitate to change the course of your company for the better. This aim is possible, plausible, and achievable by educating your teams on values, expectations, and goals, with ongoing training and commitment.

I've been brought into many already established companies tasked with building a stronger culture. Each time I start the same way—with the basics.

Identifying Strengths

As I mentioned earlier, everyone has strengths. Find out what those strengths are upfront. Often a short, formal assessment of an individual's strengths is the best way to do this.

Along with identifying the positive ways in which an employee can contribute to your company, this practice sends the message that you're committed to building on people's strengths. You're also reinforcing a culture that values strengths, without always focusing only on areas that need improvement—weaknesses. Thus you are going back to recognizing successes as opposed to only singling out failures. Both are learning experiences, but it's the positive approach that makes the difference.

Spreading the Culture

In an ideal culture and learning environment, new hires should start by learning about the company's culture, history, its vision for today and the future, and about the industry. Then comes product and equipment training.

Spending time upfront on the intangibles is important. I've already talked about the fact that they matter. They affect engagement, performance, attrition, and long-term company success.

Mentoring

One of the most positive and far-reaching approaches to learning is mentoring. The best companies have formal programs that allow their people—including new hires—to shadow someone else, to watch and learn from an expert. They have informal mentoring, too. Individuals feel comfortable simply reaching out to others for help and guidance.

I have been fortunate to have had many great mentors in my career. Each truly cared, was open and honest in his or her communications and assessments, believed in me, and pushed me to excel.

The Accountability Factor

The right culture demands employees and leadership be held accountable for actions and results, as well as for ongoing learning. That goes for the boss, too. Holding people accountable is about being proactive and continually upping the game and the goals—personally as well as companywide.

Metrics Are Important

Accountability, like other aspects of culture, again comes from the top. Quality and effectiveness are measured by concrete goals, tangible achievements, and outcomes. If you establish values, create a culture that promotes those values, set goals with strategies to achieve them, and follow through to your goals and a vision, you've built in accountability.

Accountability is about working hard to attain the right outcomes. At winning companies, everyone leads and takes ownership of their responsibilities.

Performance Reviews

As is the best practice at successful companies, performance reviews should be tied to accomplishments in terms of results and ongoing learning in your field.

Pleasanton, California-based Workday (NYSE: WDAY), a cloud-based leader in financial and human resources software, embraces this new and better approach to performance reviews. The company no longer "rates" its people. Instead, leaders focus on pointed communication and conversations with employees. This approach removes the negativity associated with ratings as part of performance.

The approach produces better, more focused results, too. People now know what they're doing right and how to improve those areas that come up short. They're held accountable, they know it, and their performance improves as a result.

Culture Check/Learning and Education

Does your company have a formal learning plan in place for its leaders and its employees? If so, what's working? What needs improvement? Remember, this is an opportunity to offer constructive suggestions and solutions.

If your company doesn't have an established learning plan to help its employees learn and grow, how might you and other team members encourage the leadership to provide it? Think about how training and education can be a win-win situation for all parties. Remember, too, that a hesitant employer is much more likely to accept small beginnings rather than grandiose ones. Lunch and learn can be an easy starting point most anywhere.

Does your company have a formal process for identifying individual strengths? Any strength assessment should be short and to the point. The goal, after all, is to identify areas in which someone excels and leverage that.

Does your company capitalize on individual strengths to strengthen the team?

If so, how might the company improve on its process? If not, why not? What can you do to encourage the right positive behavior? Again, it's about showing the win-win potential of a particular action or situation. I know I've said this before, but success is a team effort.

At your company, are leaders held accountable for creating a learning environment? Are individuals held accountable for investing in their learning and performance? In an ideal organization, people are held as accountable for their personal development as they are for their performance.

CHAPTER 10

Leaders Who Drive Operational Excellence Net Extraordinary Results

Leadership is bringing ordinary people together to achieve extraordinary results.

—*Diane K. Adams*

When everything about an organization simply works, that's operational excellence in action. The company's values-based culture is right, its operations disciplined, its people challenged, and its customers happy. The bottom line becomes exceptional results no matter the business, the circumstances, or the external economics.

Driving this kind of operational excellence are great leaders. These are individuals who embrace and promote high values, recognize the importance of innovation, and understand the cadence required for execution.

Perfect Harmony

I have been both blessed and fortunate in my career to work alongside masters of operational excellence. These are extraordinary leaders who have built some of the most successful companies and brands in the world:

- Allscripts' former leader, Glen Tullman, is an entrepreneur whose passion for solving the medical crisis in the United States led to the founding of a multimillion-dollar business and a revolution in health-care technology.

- High Point University's Nido Qubein, a refugee turned American success story, first came to America as a teenager who didn't speak a word of English. Today, everything he touches turns to gold with the help of his positive values-based approach to business and life.
- Cisco's John Chambers, an oft-honored visionary in business, technology, and world leadership, overcame dyslexia to lead Cisco, one of the most successful and enduring technology companies of the last 25 years. He's a master communicator, relationship builder, and innovator.
- SEPI Engineering's founder Sepi Saidi, an Iranian refugee, came to America for an education and overcame the odds to translate that education into founding one of the most successful small engineering companies in North Carolina. She, too, has mastered the art of communications and relationship building in business.

Beyond Command and Control

The best leaders surround themselves with a team of people who don't need them. These teams are made up of individuals who are competent, of strong character, honest, and secure enough with themselves that they don't need you to be successful.

While I was at Allscripts, for example, then-CEO Tullman had created an agile and efficient company with a strong values-based culture and values-based people. He knew we would be honest with him and get the job done. The company's culture perpetuated the important values that in turn generated effective operations.

Each of us knew our clearly defined roles, the stakes involved, the objectives, and how to collectively or individually handle any situation. Glen also knew we would always tell him the truth, and we all understood that we wouldn't be fired for it. That's operational excellence for any company, and it translates into an organization that has the ability to achieve long-term growth and success.

Common Thread

What binds Glen and other great leaders is not their brilliance for strategy or their success. Rather, it is their values and a desire to give back and make the world around them even better. They have a passion for building a culture of success, one in which individuals share a common purpose and are unleashed to reach their full potential. Their companies then can and do reach their full potential.

Numbers Tell the Story

Research shows that companies with individuals at the helm who share positive leadership behaviors produce vastly better returns than companies with weak or poor leaders. That's especially true in chaotic and uncertain economic times.

Consider a few numbers:

- Over a ten-year period through 2011, the top 20 companies for leadership (as identified by Hay Group's annual Best Companies for Leadership survey) produced nearly twice the shareholder return than that generated by the Standard & Poor's (S&P) 500—5.39 versus 2.92 percent.[1]
- The stock price of well-led companies grew 900 percent over a ten-year period, while those companies with a perceived lack of strong leadership grew only 74 percent.[2]
- Employees with good leadership work 57 percent harder and are 87 percent less likely to leave their jobs than those with poor leaders.[3]

Brad Wilson, president and CEO of Blue Cross Blue Shield of North Carolina (BCBSNC), is another exceptional leader. His company has an enviable bottom line to prove it.

In an industry marked by distrust and poor customer care, Brad has a reputation of honesty and authenticity that extends beyond simply the company. He's a motivational and inspirational visionary who sets high goals, all of which leads to extraordinary results.

During a time when many health insurers have been the brunt of public criticism, he's built up BCBSNC with the help of community outreach, health and wellness efforts, new technologies, and services. His company's nonprofit foundation has invested more than $100 million back into the community. Company community accomplishments range from funding health and wellness initiatives to providing hundreds of thousands of volunteer hours. Some examples include the following initiatives:

*Nourishing North Carolina is an initiative in partnership with the North Carolina Parks and Recreation Association to promote access to healthy foods. The goal is to establish and maintain at least one community garden in every county in North Carolina. Already, the gardens have produced more than 320 tons of produce!

*To encourage healthy outdoor lifestyles, BCBSNC funded greenways across the state, including in Wilmington and Raleigh.

*To help address the shortage of medical personnel in the state and increase educational opportunities for returning military veterans, the company funded a Physician's Assistant Master's Program in conjunction with the University of North Carolina School of Medicine.

Company profits are up, too. In 2013 alone, income at North Carolina's largest insurer was up 60 percent, revenues climbed 10 percent, and the company added 90,000 customers over the previous year.[4]

Beyond the bottom line, Wilson and his company's accolades include

- Working Mother Media: Top 100 Best Companies for Working Mothers (2007–2013—seventh consecutive year);
- The Ethisphere Institute: World's Most Ethical Company Award;
- Diversity Inc: Top 10 Company for Diversity in the South;
- American Association of Retired Persons (AARP): Top 50 Employer for Employees Over 50; and
- Carolina Parent: Top 50 Family Friendly Employers.[5]

Leadership a Big Draw

Great leaders like Brad build great cultures that in turn attract great people to their companies. Who wouldn't want to work for a leader who sets high goals, inspires and teaches his or her teams, develops two-way communications, and accomplishes winning results?

My boss at Qlik, Lars Bjork, often says it's important to hire people who are better than you are. That's how you build a good company.

I've found, too, that the No. 1 reason employees leave companies is poor leadership from their direct manager.

Remember when I talked about the negativity generated by jealousy in the workplace? I introduced you to the great leader who left one job for what he thought would be a better one on the promise of tremendous challenge and excellent leadership. Only he left the new job because of his new boss' jealousy. That was the same leader he thought would be so great.

Leadership sets the tone, lays the foundation, and proves the catalyst, good or bad.

What Makes a Great Leader?

What makes a leader like Brad or Sepi, Lars, John or Glen great? And how can you or anyone become a master of operational excellence and achieve the same kind of positive results?

It begins with that passion, drive, and intentional commitment that I've been so lucky to watch in action with great leaders. I've shared some of those passions with you throughout this book.

Five Leadership Behaviors

Beyond those inherent traits, I've identified five leadership behaviors that are accountable and measurable, and that are characteristic of great leaders across the board in any organization or industry. As a reflection of the cultures they build, great leaders

- **Put Clients and Others First.** That means always doing the right thing and not necessarily what's easiest.
- **Regularly Communicate with Teams Openly, Honestly, and without Negative Repercussions.** Success, after all, is a team effort.
- **Develop and Reward Those Teams as Part of Overall Accountability.** Accountability extends to the leadership, too.
- **Make a Difference and Achieve Results.** They're a positive force for their peers, their company, and their community.
- **Aim for Innovation in All That the Company Does.** This means they not only focus on innovative ideas, actions, and processes but do so with an eye to future success.

A leader who models these behaviors and builds them into everything his or her company does can help transform a company that's struggling or simply getting by into one with operational excellence.

Encouraging Leadership in Others

Leaders, no matter what else they do, must build the right culture and teach others how to lead. They must be clear about strategies and drive the execution. The end result then can be operational excellence.

Clarity. At Qlik, we accelerate the desired culture with set and clearly defined, in writing, specific expectations for each of our leaders. Those expectations revolve around the company's five core values—move fast, teamwork for results, open and straightforward, take responsibility, and challenge.

Operations Reviews. We reinforce positive behaviors and further cement the company's values and culture with the help of constructive operations reviews for leaders. Clarity and communications are essential, along with consistency in expectations and delivery. People want and need to know what they're doing right and what needs work.

This is a two-way process because the company promotes open communications, which includes feedback from leaders.

Most successful companies hold leadership reviews quarterly. These reviews can last several days, and attendance for leaders is mandatory. The presence of the entire team keeps everyone aligned in their actions and leads to increased productivity and results, as well as accountability.

Reviews best practices include utilizing a consistent format in which each leader presents his or her goals and achievements (or lack thereof) for the quarter. These presentations should include personal assessments in the form of charts. For example, green indicates a goal is completed successfully; yellow, completed but not so successful; and red is for incomplete. Comments correspond to the achievement level. Any goal marked red or yellow requires an action plan for achievement.

Presentations also should include goals for the following quarter, along with specific deliverables and notations of what's required to ensure completion. At the end of each presentation, the CEO should then provide his or her comments on what's good and what else others can do to improve their presentations. Then the floor should be opened for discussions and feedback.

Another best practice: record all the presentations for further review and follow-up.

This is a grueling approach to reviews, but can be well worthwhile. The presence of peers ensures that everyone on the team understands what needs to be accomplished and the deliverables required from each of them to ensure all the goals are reached.

The process may sound complex, especially for small companies, but in-depth reviews like this are essential for accountability and as a yardstick of performance.

The Big Turnaround

Peer input is essential to success. Without open and honest communication, there is no operational excellence. A chief executive—whether the company is a small operation or a worldwide behemoth—can't make the best possible decisions for the company.

Alan Mulally, former president and CEO of Ford Motor Company, and currently a member of Google's board of directors, recently recounted a great example of how this kind of feedback can literally move companies.

A number of years ago, Ford was struggling, especially with production issues. Yet every executive produced glowing reports at operations reviews. All their indicators were green, as in everything was positive and under control.

Finally, prior to one review, a leader told Alan that his plant had major production issues. Thousands of cars were held up and wouldn't ship on time. Alan told him to bring the report to the review. Instead of the all greens, this executive dared to tell the truth—he came in with all the dreaded red indicators. Everything was in trouble. His fellow executives were stunned. How would Alan react to hearing the truth?

Being the great leader that he was and is, Alan congratulated the executive on finally bringing the real issue to the table and asked for a plan to solve the problems. That in turn led to brainstorming to resolve the real issues.

Fellow executives quickly got the message that Alan wanted open and honest communications. At the next meeting, fellow executives showed up with their own straightforward evaluations of their initiatives. Openness and transparency became the norm at Ford, as did true operational excellence.

Inspire Others

Leaders at successful companies know they must set goals, own solutions, inspire, and teach others. It's a big responsibility, but it works when the culture is right at both big companies and small ones.

Remember the approach and success of SEPI Engineering and Rachel Kendall Realty? Both promote a culture with leadership that inspires others to help each other respectfully, honestly, and candidly.

Rachel Kendall and her small team huddle every morning to discuss what's top-of-mind, what needs to be done, how team members can help each other, and so on. Rachel recalled a recent morning when, after the meeting, one of her agents walked up to another and respectfully offered a bit of critical advice. Rather than rail at the advice, as is often the case at culturally misguided companies, the agent receiving the advice told the other, "Point taken. Thanks for helping me with that."

With model behavioral guidance and strong culture direction from Rachel as the team's leader, this is a company that's transparent in its operations, trustful of each other, and a stellar example of cohesiveness. This is operational excellence in motion. An added bonus from this kind of working environment, Rachel tells me, is zero attrition.

The Vision for Tomorrow

Operational excellence demands leadership with the vision to be ready to compete tomorrow, too, and with the values and expectations to make it all happen.

TechNOWism

Carlos Dominguez, the technology evangelist and innovator, refers to this kind of forward thinking in the context of today's changing business environment as "techNOWism." Says Carlos, "In a new world with new rules, you can't expect the things that made you successful in the past to be the same ones that will make you successful in the future."[6]

Well said. For leaders like Sepi, Glen, Nido, John, Brad, Rachel, Alan, and so many others, this vision for tomorrow is part of the insatiable curiosity that drives him or her to stay in tune to today, yet have the foresight to aim for something different and better tomorrow.

Status Quo Isn't Good Enough

In health care, for example, consider Brad—and his company, BCBSNC. Innovation and vision are crucial aspects of Brad's leadership. He understands that in his ever-changing business, as in any business, no matter today's successes, the status quo isn't good enough to ensure a winning tomorrow.

BCBSNC continually invests in new initiatives and directions with the future needs of its clients (subscribers and patients) and the changing health-care system in mind. It also invests millions of dollars and plenty of man-hours back into the community.

When the *Affordable Care Act* became law, an innovative BCBSNC set up mall storefronts to better reach and educate consumers on the new health-care law.

Last year, the company partnered with various health-care organizations to explore new care options for patient post-hospital stays. The stated goal is better patient care and outcomes at more reasonable prices.[7]

When It Doesn't Work

Like Brad, great leaders at long-time successful companies understand that winning leadership must be a combination of operational as well as strategic excellence.

Talk Isn't Reality

I dealt with one CEO at a growing company who insisted he was focused on developing operational excellence. But, the CEO's team didn't have the operational prowess to get the necessary pipeline in place to successfully scale his company.

In that kind of a situation, the CEO needs to step up and effectively manage his team. That means removing a strategy-only focused leader, and replacing him with someone more operational in scope. In this specific case, the CEO was unwilling to do that. Instead, the leader stayed put and so did the company. In the face of strong competition, the company lost market share. Rather than an agile company expanding on its operational excellence, the CEO was left with a company that was struggling.

After months of dropping company performance, the CEO finally real-ized he needed to be proactive and make sure his team had the operational expertise to get the job done. He reassigned the strategist and replaced him with an operational powerhouse. The company then was able to move for-ward and address its competition.

Effective Leadership Leads to Extraordinary Results

Leaders with effective performance management skills produce better results than their counterparts who lack these abilities.

Studies show effective leadership leads to better productivity, less staff turnover, greater achievement of potential, and better customer satisfaction. For example, analysis from The Ken Blanchard Companies found that

- the average organization forfeits $1 million annually in untapped potential;
- organizations generally operate with a 5 percent to 10 percent productivity loss that could be avoided with better leadership practices; and
- turnover at the average organization could drop by 9 percent by improving levels of respect, recognition, direction, and levels of support—all aspects of solid leadership.[8]

The SHRM Foundation in 2012 talked about even stronger correlations between solid leadership and better bottom lines. One study, SHRM reported, showed 50 percent less staff turnover, 10 to 30 percent higher customer satisfaction ratings, 40 percent higher employee commitment ratings, and double the net profits.[9]

The Compensation Conundrum

Effective performance management includes establishing a compensation system that's right for your people and your business. Teams should be rewarded for stellar performance. Too often companies and their leadership don't do that.

Rather, they link pay structure strictly to length of employment and/ or award bonuses arbitrarily or automatically. Both approaches do little to incentivize teams or to reflect a culture of accountability.

General compensation should be linked to performance. Top performers rightfully deserve greater rewards. Sales teams, of course, should have a commission system in place. But other employees and leaders should be fairly compensated for the right behaviors and outcomes.

If you're not sure what constitutes "fair" compensation, consider what it might cost to replace that person.

To be fair, too, you must clearly communicate expectations and how achievement or lack thereof relates to compensation. All of this ties back to setting goals and working to achieve those goals. Also, in the absence of achievement, there should be consequences. Your company's success is at stake.

I'm not talking about across-the-board firings if a goal isn't met. But if expectations are clear and teams have the tools and support they need to achieve those goals, and specific goals still aren't being met, it's time to reassess your company's culture and the performance management skills of its leadership.

The Salary-Cut Option. When economic times are tough, adjusting the bottom line via compensation cutbacks is short-sighted and not the best approach. It also may not be what's best for a company's health in the long run. A salary cut should be only a last resort.

Instead, if your company is cash-strapped, look at other ways to streamline costs. Trim the fat. Do you really need fresh potted plants delivered every month? Does everything really require overnight (and more costly) mail delivery? Do you really need to be constantly flying here or there?

Some other ways to find savings in cash-strapped times include offering employees one-time cash bonuses as opposed to permanent pay raises, or developing a merit pay program that adjusts to the marketplace. You also could look at alternatives to pay raises as rewards for employees. For example, a company might provide additional tuition reimbursements or skills training for employees, or give extra time off without pay. The latter, in the form of day- or days-long furloughs has been a popular government approach to cash shortfalls in recent years.

No one really likes a pay cut, but it is a way to save money without resorting to layoffs or detrimental cutbacks.

Quicken Gets Creative with Bonuses. When it comes to innovative ways to boost pay, Detroit-based Quicken Loans has a great strategy that gives its employees more cash and helps the community at the same time. The company financially incentivizes and rewards employees who rent or buy housing in the city of Detroit, where the company's headquarters is located. Employees earn extra money and contribute to Detroit's revitalization by moving back into the city.[10]

Communicate, Communicate, Communicate. Whatever you do in terms of salaries and benefits, though, be open and clear in your communications. Conversations on compensation need to take place in the spirit of creative and joint problem solving.

Anticipate Mistakes to Avoid Them

In pursuit of operational excellence, people may make mistakes. The most common errors are putting speed over process, trying to modify character rather than behavior, and constantly reinventing rather than creating transitions.

In a best-case scenario, identifying these areas of possible weakness upfront can help you avoid or at least minimize them down the road. In a worst-case scenario, if you still find yourself and/or your company mired in these mistakes, you can at least learn from them.

Speed over Process

I've made plenty of those mistakes—and big ones. Remember in chapter 4, when, in a hurry to make changes, I brought in new hires at a higher pay rate than their counterparts already in the company?

Rather than go through the proper processes and channels, I was in a hurry. The move cost our company a small fortune. But the lesson was learned—I've never done that again.

Modify Behavior, Not Character

Conversely, I worked with the leader whose employees were highly critical of his management, and helped him modify his behavior as opposed to changing who he was—his character.

Who we are and what each of us brings to the table is what creates a dynamic, innovative workplace. Operational excellence is grown and developed by a group of dynamic individuals—exceptional leaders—operating within the context of a company's culture, and its values and goals.

Transitions versus Reinventions

It's the responsibility of a great leader to provide the guidance and structure, and then support his or her employees in their jobs.

That's what Glen did at Allscripts. That's what Alan did at Ford, and that's what you must do as a leader at your company.

Recognizing Stretch Goals

Yet another way in which great leaders build teams that can be successful is by knowing when to push employees out of their comfort zones in pursuit of excellence. These leaders don't hesitate to encourage and mentor individuals to achieve more—to, what I refer to as, *extraordinize* their lives.

One of my first jobs was as an intern with the National Institute of Environmental Health Sciences, a subsidiary of the National Institutes of Health. My boss truly believed in me and saw that I could achieve so much more. He encouraged me to stretch my goals and reach higher. His approach worked. He heard about a leadership position in another company and talked me into taking it, mentoring me along the way. He set me up for success.

I was lucky. I had a leader who understood the value of leadership training and of mentoring, and what both of those can do for those with leadership potential.

What to Look for in Potential Leaders

Netflix, another leader in its industry and in terms of great places to work, came up with a list of traits for "The Rare Responsible Person." Those traits, combined with a few others, typify a great potential leader:

- self-motivated
- self-aware
- self-disciplined
- acts like a leader
- doesn't wait to be told what to do
- never feels "that's not my job"
- picks up trash from the floor
- behaves like an owner[11]

Training Is Not a Disposable "Perk"

Companies must understand that leadership training is a necessity in good and tough economic times. As I mentioned above, the average company forfeits more than $1 million annually in untapped potential because of the lack of effective leadership.

Leadership Summit

While I was at Allscripts, the company created an innovative way to motivate, align, and invest in the development of its leaders. In addition to ongoing training, the company annually brought its leaders from around the globe together for a leadership summit. It was quite a feat, but an important and highly successful one.

Serious Business. Leaders had prereading requirements, and then-CEO Chambers, in a prerecorded video, talked about the impact of leadership. The leaders were given assessments of their strengths, too, which reinforced the importance of building on people's strengths and creating a culture that values strengths, as opposed to always focusing on areas that need improvement.

Reinforcing the Basics. I remember the first summit. William Arruda, an expert on personal branding, taught us about crucial conversations and behavioral interviewing. This material may sound like a bit much, especially for those already in leadership positions, but it wasn't. Understanding both helps leaders have the right conversations among peers and direct teams, as well understand how to hire top talent who are great culture matches, all of which are components necessary for any company to achieve operational excellence.

Each of us also was given a flip camera, to encourage video communications as a way of fostering personal communications. Despite the company's meteoric growth, personal interaction still mattered. It's essential to motivate and inspire your teams.

The bottom line was that this kind of operational excellence would (and did) accelerate the company's growth.

You Can Do It, Too

Your company may not be large enough or have the luxury of devoting several days to nothing but leadership assessments. But no matter the size of your company, you can build a great culture and encourage leadership excellence, both of which lead to sustained growth.

Define Expectations

After you've identified the values that are important, the next step in aiming for leadership excellence is defining your expectations based on those values. Those expectations could be a few key behaviors that you would like (and expect) your leaders to exhibit.

After all, the goal is to create an environment in which the defined culture is pervasive in everything your company and its people do.

Concrete Examples. For example, with open communications, focus on what your leaders can do to model and perpetuate open and honest two-way communications. Keep everyone informed and on track toward achieving the same goals.

Start by requiring regular and frequent staff meetings. Include discussions about what's top-of-mind for teams and how those actions relate to specific company goals. Require written follow-up, too.

Also, regularly require leadership to issue internal memos with the latest update on current issues and concerns. Again, this process is about maintaining focus. That is especially important for small companies, in which their nimble nature—the ability to quickly affect change—often is their competitive advantage.

Meeting in a Box (MIAB). Qlik isn't small, but as with any other business, maintaining focus on the right goals is essential.

To help leaders address all the top-of-mind issues and other essentials at meetings, I regularly send out a Meeting in a Box. Remember, that's the electronic outline/meeting guide with details of what's important now, clear expectations of deliverables, and so on that I mentioned earlier.

Culture Check/Leadership

Now, let's look at the leadership at your company. Remember, culture comes from the top. If you want a long-term successful company, it starts with the leaders.

The search for potential leaders in your company should be ongoing. After all, living the value of learning is about continually developing your teams and its members.

To help identify potential leaders, ask the following questions about each person:

- *Does the person have the ability to care, motivate, and inspire others? Can he or she rally others? That ability is inherent in true leaders.*
- *Can the individual communicate clear expectations no matter what? A leader must be able to understand and live a company's culture, and he or she must also be able to clearly convey to others kudos as well as areas that need improvement.*
- *Is the person a team player? I've said this before, but it's essential as an ingrained aspect of a successful values-based culture: success is a team effort.*
- *Does he or she have a positive approach? Both positivism and negativism are contagious. Winning companies and their leaders exude positive energy.*

There are no losers, either, only those who haven't yet achieved their full potential.

- **Is the individual open and receptive to feedback? Does the person willingly take feedback and make changes as a result?** *I look for people who take feedback and learn from it. Think about the leader who didn't want to hear the results of his 360-degree feedback. Initially, he wouldn't even engage in a conversation.*

How do your company's leaders stack up? Identifying solid leadership requires an assessment similar to that of identifying potential leaders. Pay careful attention when it comes to small companies. With fewer leaders, one mistake can have a broader impact that's tougher to correct.

PART III

Being Intentional

CHAPTER 11

My 7 Points to Culture
System of Success!

A values-based culture is the foundation for your long-term success.
—Diane K. Adams

Now that you know what a great culture looks like, the essential elements that make it great, and how culture clearly is the differentiator in the long-term success or lack thereof in an organization, it's time to take the next step.

Get ready to focus on my 7 Points to Culture, your seven-point guide to implementation of a positive values-based culture in your business. When all points are aligned, ongoing, and intentional in all aspects of your organization, you can create a high-performing company with built-in long-term growth. Your people will be energized no matter the industry or external economics, and you'll have the very best culture in which your people, your business, and the community thrive. The 7 Points to Culture include the following:

- 1: Define Your Cultural Values and Behaviors
- 2: Communicate, Communicate, Communicate
- 3. Integrate Your Values into All Aspects of Your Company
- 4: Drive Culture through Leadership
- 5: Show You Care: Engage and Invest in Your Team
- 6: Give Back: Make a Difference beyond the Workplace
- 7: Make It Fun: Reward, Recognize, and Celebrate

Let's look more closely at how and why this approach can work for you.

The Right Culture as Your Reality

Too often, companies and their leaders say they understand the importance of a positive culture, yet implementation falls short. Sometimes it's the fear factor prompted by the perceived cost or the idea of failure. Or, some leaders simply can't embrace the open and honest interchange that must go along with teamwork to create a successful culture.

Other times, it's a lapse in judgment or values that gets lost or forgotten amid the pressures of a competitive, profit-centric environment. Leaders, too, can overlook one or more of the essential 7 Points to Culture.

The seven points intertwine the essential values of successful companies that I've discussed throughout the book with the concept of satisfied employees and customers.

Let's revisit those essential values:

- *Integrity and respect*
- *Innovation*
- *Communication and collaboration*
- *Customer success*
- *Giveback/social responsibility*
- *Learning is your edge; invest in your people.*
- *Leaders who drive operational excellence net extraordinary results.*

You must pay attention to all these values and intertwine them with the 7 Points to Culture to develop a strong foundation for your own culture success.

This Approach Really Works

Even if you've tried other approaches to culture and come up short, this approach works when others don't because of the power of total alignment of strategy. The 7 Points to Culture is your checklist to ensure that alignment. True culture, after all, is pervasive. All the essential values must be a part of everything a company, its leaders, and its teams say and do.

Without that total alignment—if just one value is overlooked or one point forgotten—a culture will miss the mark. Even if the value is unintentionally forgotten or the action is done accidentally, a positive culture can't survive long term without *all* the values and *all* 7 Points to Culture working in tandem.

A Business Initiative

Don't be overwhelmed by the enormity of the idea of developing and implementing this kind of culture.

Develop a VSE. Building a great culture is like any other business initiative and should be approached as such – intentionally and with commitment. That means, you must develop your VSE. Remember this concept from chapter 2—Vision, Strategy, Execution.

Start by establishing a *long-range vision or goal* to be achieved. In this case, it relates to the culture you want for your company and the values you would like to go along with it.

Then develop and lay out a *strategic plan* for implementation. Your strategies should directly relate to the achievement of your vision, and also serve to measure success along the way.

Next, you're ready for the *execution*, the actual carrying out of the strategies with the vision in mind.

Write Down Your VSE. Make sure all of your leaders have a copy of the VSE nearby. Post the VSE, too, especially if you're a smaller company. Then there will be no question that everyone knows what's top of mind and what must be accomplished in a given time period.

With a VSE in place, you can avoid the disconnect between actions and goals, and ensure that leaders and employees stick to the plan. In other words, there's less likelihood someone will expend wasted energy on an objective or idea that doesn't contribute to the primary company goal.

Again, keep in mind the following:

- Vision: the long-term, overarching outlook/goal
- Strategy: an overarching plan of action that includes goals that need to be accomplished in the short term, with an eye to achieving a long-term vision
- Execution: delivering on the strategies to achieve the vision

The Secret Weapon. What makes a VSE work is that not only does it provide direction but it's also a one-page document that clearly spells out the company's values, current vision related to those values, strategy to achieve that vision, and the very specific goals required for success. It's your measuring stick.

THE VSE PROCESS

To help ensure the success of your business initiatives, take the VSE approach. Establish a Vision, lay out Strategies to achieve the vision, and then launch formal Execution, those actions needed to complete the business initiative.

Here's your VSE Worksheet, along with some questions to consider:

- *Your VISION: What is the overarching goal? What does a business initiative hope to accomplish?*
- *Your Strategy: How will you accomplish that Vision? What are the stages and actions necessary to get it done and how will you do them?*
- *The Execution: What is the subset of actions that must be completed in line with the specific strategy?*

Follow this process to implement your values and get culture right, and you'll vastly enhance your company's opportunity for success.

Off the Mark

Consider the once giant Kodak. With its little brown-box film camera that brought photos to the masses as a base, Kodak had a lock on the film photography industry. The company figured its future success was assured.

Rather than embrace innovation and pay attention to the shifting demographics of its potential customer base, Kodak continued to rely on its tried-and-true products and marketing approach. Even as digital photography took over the space—and even though Kodak held one of the first patents on the digital camera—the company failed to reinvent itself in time. Kodak declared bankruptcy in 2012.[1]

Such is the importance of the pervasive nature of all the essential values in a culture. Kodak overlooked innovation and customer success, and paid the ultimate price.

Winning Combination

Online retailer Amazon.com is a sharp contrast to Kodak. Under the guidance of CEO Jeff Bezos, the company's culture is future focused—an essential ingredient for innovation. The company's success then becomes a combination of what innovation guru Carlos Dominguez calls the delivery mentality and the discovery outline.

Amazon is a model of operational excellence that is reinforced by its customers' positive experiences—the delivery mentality. The company continuously reinvents itself, too—the discovery outline – with the newest products and services. Think about Amazon's Kindle reader morphing into the Kindle mobile phone, Amazon's newest foray into same-day home grocery delivery, and so on.

Kodak, on the other hand, sat on its aging laurels.

Plausible Reality

People tend to think that culture is complicated. But it's not, especially if you approach it as the business initiative it is and with a VSE. However, it is a big investment in terms of commitment to your values, your team, your customers, and the future of your organization.

I remember a specific situation in which Allscripts had just merged with a chief competitor. Imagine two rivals with two different attitudes and two different ways of doing everything, suddenly combined into one entity and expected to work seamlessly. That was the setting when I joined the company to lead its culture and talent team.

It was as if arch-rivals Pepsi and Coca-Cola suddenly joined forces. As you can imagine, breaking down serious behavioral differences was no easy task. The secret to success, however, lay in Allscripts' values-based culture that served as the foundation for building and melding both sales forces into one cohesive unit.

The culture modeled by Allscripts, its leaders, and its employees, provided a template of values and actions for the new teams to follow. With that solid foundation, it became much easier to align all 7 Points to Culture.

The process worked, too. With the help of our CLEAR communications strategy, everyone understood the vision, strategies, and execution that were necessary across the entire company. From a success perspective, in three years we scaled from a $500 million company to $1.44 billion.

Culture Check/7 Points to Success

The 7 Points to Culture intertwine with the essential values of successful companies to create engaged employees and satisfied customers. Both lead to long-term successful growth for a company.

Are your company's values inherent in everything? Are they reflected in employees' and leaders' actions, as well as customer interactions? They should be. Culture, after all, is pervasive.

Does your company have a VSE or a similar approach that clearly spells out visions, strategies, and execution for all participants? This is an approach that constantly and consistently keeps everyone working with the same values and toward the same goals.

Create your company's own VSE today by making the commitment and taking the time to do so. That means open and honest communications at all levels, the sharing of ideas and options, and then the development of an approach that works.

CHAPTER 12

Make It Happen

Success is the intersection of preparation and opportunity.

—*Diane K. Adams*

Now it's your turn to set yourself and your company up for the same high level of culture success as the winning companies I've talked about throughout this book.

With the 7 Points to Culture system of success as your guide, you can make it happen. Keep in mind, this approach is about total long-term success and must be pervasive. The 7 Points to Culture is a total buy-in package. It's proven, and it works. If you truly commit to the total package—to approach the developing of your culture as any other business initiative with a concrete Vision, Strategies, and Execution—you WILL reap the rewards.

That means you must establish your Vision, the values for your company; devise Strategies, the steps to achieve deliverables; and follow through with Execution. Then, you can come out a winner.

Let's look closer at implementation of each of the 7 Points to Culture and take a business initiative approach to getting it right.

Point 1: Define Your Cultural Values and Behaviors

Culture is the values that drive your organization and its teams' thinking and actions all the time. It literally is your company's persona, and it starts from the top—from the CEO, boss, big guy, or whatever the title associated with the chief in your company.

This is an opportunity to make sure the values you and your team see as important for your company really are, and that they become a real part of everyday operations and actions.

Often, positive values are overlooked or forgotten in favor of emotional decisions and/or quick profits.

Assess the Important Behaviors

You define values for a business just as you do in your personal and family life—by first assessing the behaviors that are important and then clearly spelling them out.

In my family, for example, we clearly defined the values that matter to us. They're even posted on the wall in our den. And we do our best to live those values, just as you want your company and employees to live the values.

Getting There. First, the CEO or boss must sit down with his or her leaders in the company to talk about the values he or she feels are important *and* the rationale behind them. Whatever the size of a company, this is about determining what matters—those values and behaviors that are important to your company's long-term success. That takes open and honest discussions.

Importance of Feedback. This is communications on steroids. If yours is a big company, engage the full executive team and get feedback. If your company is small, you still need a formal assessment procedure that solicits input from others. Gather the leaders first for discussions, then bring in the next layer down for further discussions, and so on.

When I was at Allscripts, to ensure our values matched our growing company, we sat down as an executive team off-site and had hard conversations about our strengths and weaknesses, what was right and what we needed to change as a company.

The same kind of discussions happened at Qlik as the company evolved from a small start-up into a burgeoning powerhouse and faced the challenge of scaling successfully. The executive team met, and we talked about redefining the behaviors that were important and what we needed to do to accelerate our growth.

To Scale Successfully. In both cases, the premise for discussions was simply to define what mattered. That's a premise that works for every company.

Keep in mind, too, that organizations need to make the time for this all-important self-analysis in order to scale successfully.

Some issues and questions to consider in your company's discussions include the following:

- Why do the values in general matter; why does a specific value matter?
- What are the expectations related to each value in terms of leaders, team members, and beyond?
- How will those expectations be integrated into actions and behaviors?
- How should expectations be reflected in the company's policies and procedures?

From Discord to Agreement. If there's disagreement among leaders and participants—likely there will be—keep talking until you have agreement. After all, values must be pervasive, and that means a buy-in by all parties.

We all know the negative consequences that can result when a company claims it has high values, yet the actions of its leaders tell a far different story. Think about Enron. As I mentioned earlier, Enron's lofty values were chiseled in stone at the company headquarters, yet its executives' behaviors modeled something else entirely. The company collapsed amid scandal, fraud, and lies.

Honest Evaluations

How long has it been since you've evaluated your organization's underlying values? If it's been a while, it's time to revisit them. Or, if you're not who you want to be as a company, it's time to revisit those values.

Even if your company is doing great but wants to get better, take another look at those values and what matters. Question each one. Do they truly reflect the most important values for your company?

Often, a misaligned or misguided culture can be, in part, the result of a disconnect between a perceived value and its implementation, or the perceived value may not exist at all, with something else entirely in its place.

Think about the boss who, busy with other things, assumes his or her company is working perfectly. Then, for whatever reason, one day he runs head-on into the fact that the company or a division of the company is in chaos. That happens more often that you think when communications have broken down or are nonexistent.

To be fair, without vigilance communications easily can break down over the years. Especially at large companies, the boss (or the C-suite) can lose track of what's real and what's perceived as real. Don't let that happen at your company. Make the effort to pay attention to the details.

Sound Foundation

This is your opportunity to make sure your company lays the right foundation for success. Make the most of the opportunity by addressing the important issues upfront. The most successful companies get input on issues from bosses, leaders, and employees. The latter, after all, know the customers best.

Test the relevance of a perceived value with your team members. Do they think it matters? Again, your perceptions as a leader may differ from the day-to-day reality. That's OK at this stage of culture building. This kind of feedback and buy-in now will only strengthen clarity on the values of real importance and ensure a better culture later.

More questions and issues to address honestly include the following:

- How do those values you feel are important to your company impact customers and the community?
- Are those values shared by all your leaders? What about your staff? If not, why not?
- Do those values reflect your company's mission statement? (Do you even have a mission statement? If not, it's time to develop one.)
- Does your company's culture manifest those values? If not, why not and what's missing?
- If not, could it be because your perception of a company value is off or your team's perception is wrong?
- Is a particular value even relevant to your business?

Get the Values in Writing

Be sure to write down responses and conclusions related to the values that matter. These will become the building blocks to help your company and its people achieve excellence.

As always, there are no right answers because every company and every situation is different.

Unsure of What Matters?

If you're not sure what values really matter for your company, start by evaluating the 7 Essential Values of Successful Companies. How might any or all of those values relate to your company, its products or services, the community, and so on?

Those values include the following:

- **Integrity and respect.** This includes fostering an all-inclusive workplace.
- **Innovation.** Winning companies promote discovering new and better ways of thinking and of accomplishing goals.
- **Open communication and collaboration.** Success is a team effort; everyone is a contributor.
- **Customer success.** Your company's success is a natural outgrowth of your customers' success.
- **Giveback/social responsibility.** Giving back to others fosters long-term loyalty through good and bad economic times.
- **Learning is your edge; invest in your people.** Ongoing employee learning and education pay dividends because your employees' growth fuels your company's growth.
- **Leaders who drive operational excellence net extraordinary results.** Culture comes from the top, and so does operational excellence. Great leaders develop great companies with great cultures.

Don't be surprised if, in frank and open discussions with your team, you discover a value that is of importance to your company that's not on the list.

Point 2: Communicate, Communicate, Communicate

Once you've identified the values that are important to you and your company, it's time to communicate them to everyone in your company.

Get the Word Out

Communicate means more than offering a single sentence that says, "This is the value; do it." Communications consists of truly and intentionally conveying the all-important values to every person in your company—from leaders down to the lowest-level employee.

Firing off a quick memo or a blast email that says we've come up with six or seven values that should be reflected in everything our company does, and expecting everyone to immediately incorporate the values into all their actions is not enough, nor is only telling this to the sales chief or marketing guru and expecting him or her to pass it on to other team members.

You need to convey each of your company's values and why it should be part of everyday operations. Achieving total adoption requires plenty of repetition and reminders. The value has to have a chance to become a part of every action.

(Don't forget the T-shirt ploy, either. That was Glen Tullman's measure of our level of innovation and how great our culture was while I was at Allscripts.)

To do this demands an explanation of a value, the reasoning behind it, and the expected positive outcomes as a result. Develop a strategy for doing this.

Consider the value of customer success, which is about making sure your customers' problems, no matter what they are, are solved. This value requires more than selling a customer on your product to fulfill a sales quota when you know it's not the best fit for his or her needs, telling a customer you can't solve his or her problem, or dismissing a customer's complaint as worthless or unfounded.

Customer success means doing everything possible—going the extra mile—to help the customer be successful, whether there's a sale in it for you or not. This value is about always being gracious, honest, and kind to customers and helping them solve their individual problems no matter how unrelated they might be to your level of expertise or product. The value also means always trying your best to model the right behavior and provide your team with the training and tools they need to excel in solving customer issues.

A happy customer, after all, is a satisfied customer and will likely come back, or at the very least, recommend you and your company to others.

Company-wide introduction. An all-hands meeting led by the CEO or boss is a great way to clearly convey the company's commitment to this kind of a values-based organization. It also reinforces a tone of commitment.

Follow-up. Follow-up should include modeling ALL the desired values-based behaviors as well as reinforcing the company values whenever possible—at the outset of meetings, in communications, electronic or otherwise, and posted online and in the physical workspace.

Qlik CEO Lars Bjork intentionally highlights specific company values at every all-hands meeting. All of our leaders make it a point to reinforce those same values at other times, too.

Recognition doesn't cost anything. However, receiving the honor of having people pay attention to outstanding performance makes a big difference for employees and is a big motivator. When people see others recognized for their values and behavior, it becomes clear what actions are important to the company.

Overcoming Resistance

If a value is new to your company and/or workplace, pay attention to and prepare for resistance to change. This is a normal human reaction. It could be prompted by the "if it's not broken, why fix it" mentality, or simply be a matter of someone's not being amenable to change.

Positive Reinforcement. Positive reinforcement for the right behaviors in the form of recognition and reward can often solve the problem. Also, be sure to introduce the expected change in the context of how it can improve the individual employee's or leader's work life.

For example, with the Qlik value of moving fast, the strategy is designed to create better outcomes. That in turn means less wasted time and effort by team members and happier customers, because we're solving their issues. Better outcomes mean quotas are more easily satisfied, lessening the pressure on individuals to perform.

Peer Recognition. At Strata Decisions in Chicago, peer recognition is a strong motivator for the company's stated value of social responsibility/giveback. On the wall in the company's break room is a sign-up sheet for volunteer activities, along with comments and photos of employees involved in social giveback.

There's also a Wall of Fame at the company's entrance that is packed with huge photos, and that, again, recognizes employees who go the extra mile.

Leadership Praise. Qlik holds an all-hands meeting once a quarter with everyone in attendance—in person or via technology links. At every meeting, Lars recognizes several individuals for their outstanding commitment to a particular aspect of the company's stated values-based culture. These are people who are nominated by their peers for their performance, and their accomplishments are posted online on Qlik's Wall of Fame.

You Can Do It, Too

Any organization of any size easily can provide a similar kind of recognition for team members whose actions exemplify company values. Call out the individual during a team meeting, honor that person on a Wall of Fame (virtual or otherwise), and if you want to provide extra incentive, offer a small gift card or other compensation for a job well done.

With the value of customer success, for example, you could celebrate once a week or once a month the best customer service provided by an employee. I've seen some companies recognize employees by passing around a commemorative trophy or a similar item. My local grocery features its Employee of the Month on a huge wallboard at the store's entrance.

It's the behavior, the honor, and the peer recognition that matter. When culture comes alive and team members model positive behavior, negative behavior has no place. Those holdouts to adopting particular values either change and accept the values or they're left behind—they are either pushed out or they end up leaving the organization.

If you've built a great culture, people who don't live those values naturally leave the organization. Zappos! actually pays nonculture-matched new employees to leave. That's how important culture is at that highly successful company.

Point 3: Integrate Your Values into All Aspects of Your Company

Every action of your company, its leaders, and its team members is a reflection of your company's values. These actions are much more than fancy statements pranced out at meetings or posted on walls.

Culture is in all of your company's and its peoples' everyday actions. Values are lived day in and day out in all the company's processes and procedures, too, whether internally among staff or externally with customers and the community.

Actions Are a Reflection of Words

Nordstrom does a phenomenal job of living its guiding value of good judgment in all situations. The value is based on its realization of the importance of its customers' success. When was the last time you heard or saw a Nordstrom associate argue with or challenge a customer? They simply don't do that.

Conversely, remember the company I worked for as a young mother that also said its peoples' personal lives counted, and yet I was so loaded down with work that it was impossible to spend any time with my family? No matter what values the company claimed mattered, the actions of its people painted a very different picture.

Power of Total Alignment

A company's words and its actions must align for culture success. That's simply the pervasive nature of culture.

Several times throughout this book I've talked about Allscripts' commitment to high values. Among the manifestations of those values are the company's efforts to create an open communications environment.

To that end, while I was at the company we established our CLEAR strategy. (Remember, CLEAR was an acronym that linked to our company's values: Client success, Leadership, Extraordinary people, Aspire, and Results)

CLEAR helped ensure the executive team communicated effectively among each other and that in turn, effective communications translated down the ranks.

To help accomplish that, we started every meeting with discussion about the CLEAR strategy, which included defining and modeling our values. We featured CLEAR posters throughout our workspaces and on our Intranet. We even had T-shirts printed with the CLEAR message.

There was no question: Allscripts was committed to CLEAR and expected everyone to buy into the company's values.

Values and Actions

To achieve alignment in values and actions, you must pay attention to the details in terms of actions and discussions. Too often companies don't do so, and a small slip-up—words said off the cuff, for example—result in serious consequences for a company.

What about the leader in the company who told the new mom that her future at the company was over because her child now came first? Whether it was said privately or in public, that's the wrong message to convey in a workplace that promotes inclusion.

All the people in a company must do their best to live and act all of the time within the values established for that company. It's not acceptable for the values to apply some of the time or for some of the people. Many times in my career as a people and talent executive, I've had to let people go who refused to live according to the culture and values established by the company.

Here are some basic examples of positive and negative behavior related to various company values. With some, the right versus the wrong approach seems simple and pretty basic. But that doesn't always mean companies or their people knowingly or unknowingly do the right thing:

- **Innovation.** Top companies encourage their teams to find new and better ways of reaching positive outcomes. **Right:** A line customer service representative immediately recognized a customer's problem and took the actions necessary to solve it. **Wrong:** At one company, when an employee suggested an alternative (and better) solution to solving a customer service issue, his superior reprimanded him for not following written procedure and for going directly to the source of the problem.
- **Giveback/Social Responsibility.** Giving back to others fosters long-term loyalty on the part of employees and customers through good and bad economic times. **Right:** A family-owned pizzeria encourages its employees to donate one day a month at a local food bank. **Wrong:** An advertising firm tells its employees to volunteer, but on their own time.
- **Learning Is Your Edge; Invest in Your People**. Ongoing employee learning and education pay dividends because your employees' growth fuels your company's growth. **Right:** A retail clothing company reimburses any of its employees when they complete college-level courses. **Wrong:** A publishing company reimburses the cost of continuing education only for a select few individuals, and only if the courses are outside working hours and directly related to the person's job.
- **Leaders Who Drive Operational Excellence Net Extraordinary Results.** Culture comes from the top, and so does operational excellence. **Right:** A leader at a small company encourages input from all his team when it comes to creating the best strategy to solve a client's problems. **Wrong:** The chief executive of a manufacturing plant rules his workers with an iron fist. No one is allowed to leave the line or the plant without his permission.

Without Alignment

Be very specific upfront in writing the values and the actions you expect from your leaders and team members. Keep the communications channels open at all times. Try to include the essential values as a part of discussion and feedback, too.

If someone still balks at living the stated values, then as I discussed earlier, you may have to take other actions, including separation. After all, it's your company's future that is on the line.

Point 4: Drive Culture through Leadership

Culture comes from the top. People look to their leaders for direction, and they follow the values and behaviors modeled by those leaders.

Living the Message

Leaders of successful companies guide their teams by truly living the values that matter in everything they say or do.

As the president of Allscripts, Lee Shapiro's actions reflected his true commitment to caring about his teams. Every member of the organization was an asset. As a mark of that respect, no matter where he was in the world, Lee always began any speech or discussion with that team by speaking in their local language.

On a smaller scale, Buck Buchanan, the founder of Lumpy's Ice Cream, has just 20 employees at the height of summer. But they're all part of what Buck says is the Lumpy's family. When one member couldn't afford a trip home, the Lumpy's family helped out.

The Wrong Message. At the other end of the spectrum is the leader who considers his employees disposable commodities.

I worked with one company in which the CEO decided layoffs were necessary. Rather than take the time to explain his decision to his team, and to offer them some help or guidance, he simply announced the terminations on a Friday afternoon with the admonition "don't show up here Monday." That Monday morning, the CEO had security posted at the doors to keep out the laid-off employees.

That kind of an approach left departing employees stunned, and demoralized those employees who remained. It also started a talent exodus that seriously threatened the business' ability to continue on the same competitive level. You could argue the business was headed downhill anyway, but the abrupt layoff hastened its demise. In the face of management that doesn't care, employees lose their desire to care, too.

Inspiring Your Teams

Great leaders, instead, know how to motivate and inspire their teams to accomplish great things. They bring the company's values and culture to life.

You can do that, too. If you think the values, live them, and act on them, and if you capitalize on communications opportunities, you can convey your message.

Remember Fab'rik and Evereve, with their ever-expanding boutiques? Both are winners despite tough economics and competition, because wherever the stores are located, their leaders try to live and teach their positive values—anchored by customer experience—and act on them. The company promises and delivers on its values, and it provides good product and great service with the customer experience top of mind.

So do Lumpy's, Allscripts, Cisco, and hundreds of more successful companies large and small that care about their values and their community, and communicate that in all they do.

Take the lead and get started now. Determine those values that matter to you and your company, and then share them in all that you do. Those values can become the foundation for your business and can sustain it even through tough times and with stiff competition.

Point 5: Show You Care: Engage and Invest in Your Team

Inspiring leadership means motivating your teams in tandem with investing in them. You have to make the time, expend the effort, and spend the money, if necessary, to engage and invest in your people. They need to know you care through your actions and commitment.

Early in my tenure at Qlik, I recognized that we could improve on our communications. With that in mind, Lars now monthly holds all-hands meeting and regularly recognizes team members for a job well done (the Qlik Wall of Fame, for example). This approach is an ongoing investment in our people.

The Basics

Sure, those kinds of things, along with motivating teams through financial and other incentives, are the basics. But those basics are often forgotten or overlooked at plenty of organizations, especially those caught up in highly competitive environments.

Your Turn

Even when applied on a smaller scale, the approach is the same. To engage and invest in your team requires reach to all locations—making sure everyone gets the message, capitalizing on technology (which includes making sure your team is trained to use your technology), and employing personal interaction (commitment and face-to-face contact from the top) to ensure success.

Team effort. Too often companies simply hand down decisions to their employees and expect compliance without explanations. But success is a team effort, which means that engaging your employees and getting the necessary buy-in and commitment from them requires providing them with the goals, strategies, and the reasoning behind the expected outcomes.

Engaged employees, after all, are more apt to accept role changes, to improve and expand skills, and to go above and beyond in terms of their jobs.

Continuing Education

True employee engagement demands continuing education and training. The latest and greatest matters, not only from an efficiency standpoint but from a psychological one, too. When you're willing to invest in your employees, they're in turn more willing to invest in you and your company. That translates to everyone involved being committed and sharing responsibilities, both strong motivators in a team environment.

Don't Just Talk about It. Fix It. Meteoric growth can temporarily get in the way of your teams' and leaders' education and training. Both are essential to keeping your people interested, engaged, and performing at their top levels.

No matter the circumstances or the competition, don't overlook the training and education of your teams. Listening forums, for example, can be a great way to help identify issues. Once the issues are out in the open, it's then up to companies and their leaders to take the necessary follow-up steps.

Help Your Teams Learn

What kind of training would benefit your teams—and your business? Specifically, consider what skill sets can your people learn that will make them better in their lives and in turn at their jobs. (Hint: A growing bottom line is the natural outgrowth of happy and engaged team members.)

How can you facilitate that training? Perhaps you can bring in an expert for a series of training sessions. Or, if yours is a small company that truly can't afford to stop business for a training session, why not consider a working lunch? Treat your team to a lunch and learn. This practice can be money well spent in terms of developing new and improved skills for employees across the board as well as enhancing morale.

Point 6: Give Back and Make a Difference beyond the Workplace

As industries and economies go through ups and downs, those companies that are socially responsible and operate in an environment that emphasizes give back are resilient and thrive. Even in the toughest times, people and customers stick with a company that genuinely cares.

Social responsibility energizes employees and leadership, too, as I've shown with facts and figures earlier.

Plenty of Payback

Social responsibility pays back a company with dividends. Companies involved in giveback thrive in good economic times and bad. Employees who volunteer and work at companies that give back are more engaged than their counterparts elsewhere. Volunteerism as a team can boost team strengths, too.

People who volunteer feel like they have a sense of purpose. Even when things are tough economically, if people give back, they hold onto the fact that they are making a difference no matter how their company is doing financially, and that's important. Customers support companies known for their community caring and volunteering, too.

For a company, the cost of giving its team members the time to participate becomes an investment in the company, its teams, and its future.

The most successful volunteer programs are company-wide days of service, according to the "Giving in Numbers: 2014 Report," an annual report on the state of corporate giving from CECP in association with The Conference Board. CECP, formerly known as the Committee to Encourage Corporate Philanthropy (http://cecp.co/), is a nonprofit coalition of CEOs from among the world's largest companies.

The report points to improved business performance among companies with growing giveback programs, too. More positive numbers from the report include the following:

- Companies that boosted their giving by more than 10 percent since 2010 increased median revenues by 11 percent.
- Pretax profits for 59 percent of those companies went up.[1]

What Project/Cause Suits Your Company?

Take the time to determine the best project and/or cause that best fits your company and its people. Choose right, and the cause can become a great team-building exercise and be fun, too.

Team Input. You'll get the greatest team participation in giveback if you ask for team input on choosing a relevant cause. Perhaps a fellow employee is fighting breast cancer and his or her team members want to support Breast Cancer Awareness. Or maybe a team member is active with the local Adoption Alliance and fellow workers wish to rally in support of that cause.

Giving back can be local, regional, national, or international. Above all, though, it must be relevant.

When my daughter Danielle was diagnosed with type I diabetes while I was at Cisco, my team decided to join the Juvenile Diabetes Walk for a Cure. That was more than a decade ago, yet Cisco still raises hundreds of thousands of dollars for the cause, and its people still participate in the annual Walk.

Founding Principle. Sometimes a cause becomes part of the founding fabric of a company or its owners. Ben & Jerry's, the ice cream people, founded their company with strong giveback principles in mind. Even though Ben and Jerry sold their company more than a decade ago, it's still dedicated to social responsibility and giveback.

Logical Connections

When trying to find the best giveback for your company, look for logical connections to the mission of your company.

Technology companies, for example, often invest in education because technology is a key enabler of education. Many years ago, Cisco implemented Network Academies. Today, the program, which helps prepare students for in-demand information and communications technology, is in hundreds of schools, both secondary and postsecondary. At Qlik, a part of our corporate vision is to "touch more than a billion lives." To that end, the company gives away its analytics software to nonprofits and to educational institutions.

Health-care companies often look to health-care options—donating equipment, providing immunizations, and so on. Blue Cross Blue Shield of North Carolina, for example, funds and participates in health and wellness programs in the community. Drugstore chain Walgreen's supports many causes, including providing immunizations in Third World countries.

Food service organizations often donate products and/or feed the hungry. This is a common approach and a successful one taken by many smaller companies. Those companies may have less deep pockets than global conglomerates, but they still have plenty of personal commitment to the communities they serve. Remember Milton's Pizza and Pasta? The owner always donates product to community events.

Beyond Specifics. Companies also may decide to leave the specifics of a giveback to their individual employees. Strata Decisions, for example, has its Mensch Day, the free time it provides for its employees to volunteer for the organization of their choosing.

Outside Help. Many outside sources—government as well as private and nonprofit—are available online and otherwise to help you and your teams develop the right cause or causes and effectively implement them.

Time and Recognition

Whatever cause or causes work for your company, it's important to give your people the time, support, and recognition they need and should get for their social responsibility.

While I was at Allscripts, the entire company designated two days a year for givebacks. One was a personal giveback day, and then on the other, leaders were required to designate specific projects for their teams. The company also recognized its employees for their volunteer efforts.

Qlik further incentivizes its top volunteers by providing them with life-changing humanitarian trips. In 2014, the trips included Haiti and Tanzania.

Extra Bonus. Volunteerism and giveback can be a big plus on a resume, too. Companies like those potential job candidates who believe in giving back to their community. That's especially true in today's hypercompetitive marketplaces.

How Much Giveback Is Enough?

The true value in giveback is not necessarily in the number of volunteer hours committed or the products or services donated—though both can be substantial. The biggest value created by social responsibility is the multiplier effect. When one person gives back, that action influences others to do the same.

Think about the "random acts of kindness" you hear about. If you're standing in line in a grocery and the person in front of you picks up the tab for your purchases, that action can often prompt you to do the same for someone else. Or, if you are at the ice cream store and someone pays it forward for you, you're likely to pay it forward for someone else. That happens all the time at Lumpy's, according to owner Buchanan.

Elements for Success

All these elements and more—especially commitment on the part of leadership—can contribute to the success or lack thereof of a giveback program in your company.

Let's review some of those essentials to help make sure that your company's giveback program has the best chance of success:

- **Company sponsored:** Even if a giveback is individual in nature, be sure your company offers its support in terms of donating dollars and/ or additional time for volunteers. That can increase the impact of any volunteering.
- **Employee input:** Best practice calls for giving your team members a voice in which causes to support. With this approach, they'll be more likely to commit to and give more of their time and effort.

- **Time off:** Companies must consciously give employees time off for the purpose of giveback. That takes companies making a conscious commitment to social responsibility. It's not good enough to expect team members to do their giveback during vacation time!

- **Team effort:** A team volunteer effort can be the best possible approach to team building. Work with your employees to help them identify the giveback activity that will reap the most benefit for your company—your teams will learn how to work together successfully and accomplish something positive at the same time. It's a win-win situation, and makes more sense than team-building exercises like hiking or crawling in the mud (seriously!) for fun.

- **Total participation:** If your company has multiple locations, develop a giveback activity in which everyone can participate. You can get the entire company involved if you designate specific individuals to be in charge of the giveback at the various locations. Remember how Allscripts had its culture ambassadors on-site and in charge of promoting the company's culture?

- **Showcase and recognition:** Praise and recognize your teams for their volunteer and giveback efforts. We're all little kids at heart and enjoy earning praise. Consider posting pictures, names, and volunteer activities on a company Intranet or even a physical bulletin board at your organization. Take the time to mention volunteers and their accomplishments at company meetings, and even provide incentives in the form of rewards for the most giveback hours or the best use of volunteer time, or some other honor. Let peers decide who wins the extra incentive.

- **Make it fun:** Volunteering can be rewarding and fun not only for the volunteers but for the company in general. Fundraising efforts promote camaraderie as well as a good cause. They develop a team's ability to work together toward a common goal at the same time. At Allscripts, for example, the company designated the Juvenile Diabetes Research Foundation as its cause and developed all kinds of fundraisers. There were competitions among departments and offices to raise the most money, pancake breakfasts with executives flipping the flapjacks, car washes and bake sales courtesy of employees and their families, and much more.

Point 7: Make It Fun: Reward, Recognize, and Celebrate

Just as volunteering should be fun, so should work and the workplace. That's not a novel concept. This idea is essential to the long-term success of a business.

Some organizations think that if they've hired the right people and they're aligned in their thinking and actions, that's enough. This may be true in the short term. But to sustain growth over the long haul takes more. Workplaces at successful companies have a certain amount of fun built in, as in rewards, recognition, and camaraderie.

Make the Time

In today's competitive and profit-driven business environment, not enough companies take the time to celebrate. Instead, when public or private companies start cutting costs to meet goals, the "fun" shifts to fretting about numbers.

What happens in the absence of fun? As discussed earlier in the book, employee engagement slips and attrition goes up, as does absenteeism. Production ends up suffering.

To avoid that harmful lapse requires a combination of living your company's essential values as well as paying attention to the fun factor. Seriously.

Serious Business

Serious fun makes a difference. With the right leadership and processes ingrained in day-to-day business, employees actually can enjoy coming to work. What a concept!

Remember Sepi Saidi, founder and owner of SEPI Engineering? One of her essential goals is to actually make sure she enjoys going to work every day. She works hard to help ensure her fellow workers feel the same way.

When I was at Allscripts, we worked hard at fun, too. We planned all types of events, from pie-throwing contests to ease workload tensions to contests among departments and leaders, participation in nonprofit walks, and more.

At Qlik, we work to do the same. There's strong engagement by team members relative to HopeHIV as well as ongoing recognition and reward related to everyday accomplishments. Earlier, I talked about how Lars, Qlik's CEO, regularly honors outstanding team members who truly represent the company's values.

Win-Win for All Parties

People love to be part of a winning team. It doesn't matter whether it's a team of volunteers, fellow workers, or a sports team.

Why not capitalize on that for the benefit of others and help your company in the process? You will promote camaraderie, teamwork, and culture. You reinforce positive actions and teamwork, overcome resistance to what can sometimes be difficult changes, and ensure continued adherence to the company's culture in the process, too.

It's Not That Difficult

Fun and reward don't necessarily have to cost your company anything extra. Recognition is free, and so is fun. But both can add plenty to bottom lines.

I've shown with numbers and anecdotes throughout this book how engaged and satisfied employees are better producers, how they are less likely to quit their jobs (lower job turnover equates to reduced hiring costs), and how they can help perpetuate a company's long-term success.

Think about ways in which you can ease the pressure in your workplace and make accomplishing the job more fun. This is not cutting back on expectations. This is about looking at ways to encourage camaraderie, teamwork, and high performance. The three do go together. And, they don't have to require cash outlay.

It can, however, prove costly if you don't work at making a workplace more enjoyable and your employees feel valued. It starts with commitment to a values-based culture.

How to Make Your Workplace Fun

At Qlik, we approached the rollout of a new product—a key business initiative—in a unique and fun way.

According to our VSE, the **Vision** was to have every employee understand and be able to communicate the benefits of our new product, QlikSense. To that end, our **Strategy** called for training each person in the new product. We wanted the **Execution** to be fun, so every one-hundredth person who completed the short tutorial and certification, won $100. Every one of those people donated the money, either giving it to a charity or to a peer who was doing a great job.

That's a fun way to achieve a business objective with complete company-wide engagement.

Don't be misled by the word fun. This strategy is serious business and should be approached as another business initiative.

Think VSE. What's the overarching Vision—your far-reaching goal? Perhaps, it's that you want employees to enjoy their work or experience contentment with their jobs. What are the Strategies you can lay out to achieve that Vision? After determining that, follow through step-by-step with the Execution of the Strategies.

Culture Check/Creating Your Culture Reality

Now go back through each of the 7 Points to Culture in this chapter. Once you understand all seven points and how they intertwine with your company's values, you're well on your way to creating a positive values-based culture with strong potential for ongoing growth and success for your company.

Epilogue

*N*ow that you understand what it takes to create and sustain a
great culture, and you have the tools to get there—my 7 Points to
Culture system for success—it's time to mold a great culture for your
company.

If you're starting from scratch or redefining an existing culture, this book
and my approach are about enabling companies and their people to experience
extraordinary success. I hope these pages have helped you understand how easy
and inexpensive it can be to truly live and sustain a positive values-based culture
in your company.

Whether yours is a company of 4, 40, 400, 40,000, or more, you can do
it. A great culture is achievable. It simply takes courage, commitment, and the
intentional effort to make a difference. The rewards are huge—sustained success
personally and professionally.

As I've said, culture is the game-changer. It's what sets the stage for a company's long-term success (or failure) no matter external economics.

In a competitive environment, in good economic times and bad, successful
companies are those that are intentional about establishing positive values and
living those values; that practice open and honest communications and collaboration; that truly subscribe to customer success; that pay attention to giveback; that
value what their team members contribute; and that value and give back to their
employees and their communities.

If you pay attention to those clear values that matter, if they become pervasive
in all that you and your company do, and if you follow the 7 Points to Culture,
you're well on the way. Now is your time to "extraordinize" your company and
your life.

Good luck. Let's get started together.

Find out more about culture and how to build a business culture that works for everyone by visiting my website, www.DianeKAdams.com. You can click on the icon "It Takes More than Casual Fridays and Free Coffee," to access the online workbook, too.

Notes

Introduction

1. "Stock-market Performance of Fortune 'Best 100 Companies to Work for in America'", ©2015 Russell Investments.

1   Culture: Why You Should Care

1. iFranchise News, The Rachel Kendall Team Ranked Fifth In Keller Williams Realty's Carolina Region (October 11, 2014), ifranchisenews.com, http://ifranchisenews.com/the-rachel-kendall-team-ranked-fifth-in-keller-williams-realtys-carolina-region/.
2. SHRM Foundation Executive Briefing, Employee Engagement: Your Competitive Advantage, shrm.org, www.shrm.org/about/foundation/products/documents/engagement%20briefing-final.pdf.
3. Steve Crabtree, Worldwide, 13% of Employees Are Engaged at Work (October 8, 2013), Gallup.com, www.gallup.com/poll/165269/worldwide-employees-engaged-work.aspx.
4. Corporate Executive Board's Corporate Leadership Council, Driving Performance and Retention through Corporate Engagement: A Quantitative Analysis of Effective Engagement Strategies, USC.edu, www.usc.edu/programs/cwfl/assets/pdf/Employee%20engagement.pdf.
5. SHRM Foundation Executive Briefing, Employee Engagement: Your Competitive Advantage, www.shrm.org, www.shrm.org/about/foundation/products/documents/engagement%20briefing-final.pdf.
6. Paul Rogers, Paul Meehan, and Scott Tanner, Building a Winning Culture (2006), Bain.com; http://www.bain.com/Images/BB_Building_winning_culture.pdf, pp. 1–3.
7. Ben & Jerry's, Our History, www.benjerry.com/about-us.
8. Lumpy's Ice Cream, www.youtube.com/watch?v=YW4csMrSRvg.
9. Herb Kelleher, as quoted by Ann Rhoades (www.Peopleink.com) in a presentation, Built on Values, to SHRM Foundation: Investing in the Future of HR; https://shrm.org/about/foundation/products/Documents/Rhoades%20Pres.pdf.

2 Are You Living a Double Life?

1. NPR, Tamara Keith, Decade in Review: Corporate Scoundrels and Scandals (December 31, 2009), npr.org, www.npr.org/templates/story/story.php?storyId =122083807.
2. Christopher Helman, How EOG Resources Became One of America's Great Oil Companies, Forbes, (August 12, 2013), forbes.com, www.forbes.com /sites/christopherhelman/2013/07/24/how-an-enron-cast-off-became-one-of -americas-great-oil-companies/.
3. Robert G. Eccles, Ioannis Ioannou, and George Serafeim, The Impact of a Corporate Culture of Sustainability on Corporate Behavior and Performance (2011), Harvard Business School Working Knowledge, hbswk.hbs.edu, http:// hbswk.hbs.edu/item/6865.html.
4. John H. Fleming and Jim Harter, Gallup Business Journal (December 15, 2001), Optimize, http://www.gallup.com/businessjournal/781/optimize.aspx.
5. Steve Schaefer, Yahoo Rallies after Reaping Alibaba Riches, *Forbes*, (October 21, 2014), forbes.com, www.forbes.com/sites/steveschaefer/2014/10/21/yahoo-earnings-mayer-alibaba/.
6. What's Yahoo Worth Now that Alibaba Is Public? *Fortune*, (September 22, 2014), fortune.com, http://fortune.com/2014/09/22/whats-yahoo-worth-now -that-alibaba-is-public/
7. Marketwatch, Yahoo! Inc. (May 7, 2015); www.marketwatch.com/investing /stock/YHOO.
8. Tor Dahl and Associates, Principles of Productivity, www.tordahl.com/principles .html.
9. Hay Group, Viewpoint Issue 3 (June 2010), *Getting Engaged*, haygroup.com, www.haygroup.com/downloads/ca/ViewPoint_issue_3_June_2010.pdf.
10. Matthew L. Maciejewski, Daryl Wansink, Jennifer H. Lindquist, John C. Parker, and Joel F. Farley, Health Affairs, Value-Based Insurance Design Program in North Carolina Increased Medication Adherence But Was Not Cost Neutral, healthaffairs.org, http://content.healthaffairs.org/content/33/2/300.abstract.
11. WRAL.com, Blue Cross Profits, Executive Pay Up in 2013 (February 28, 2014), WRAL.com, www.wral.com/blue-cross-profits-executive-pay-up-in-2013 /13438661/.

3 The Little Things Make a Big Difference

1. Quicken Loans, *"Fast Fact,"* quickenloans.com, www.quickenloans.com/press -room/fast-facts/.
2. Annamarie Mann and Ryan Darby, Should Managers Focus on Performance or Engagement?, Business Journal, Gallup.com (August 5, 2014), businessjournal. gallup.com, http://businessjournal.gallup.com/content/174197/managers-focus -performance-engagement.aspx.
3. Annamarie Mann and Ryan Darby, Should Managers Focus on Performance or Engagement?, Business Journal, Gallup.com (August 5, 2014), businessjour-nal. gallup.com, http://businessjournal.gallup.com/content/174197/managers -focus-performance-engagement.aspx.

4. Aberdeen Group, Analyst Insight (2013), *The Power of Employee Recognition*, aberdeen.com, http://aberdeen.com/launch/report/perspective/8750-AI-employee-recognition-program.asp.

5. Kim E. Ruyle, SHRM Webcast (July 17, 2012), Inventive Talent Consulting LLC, *Measuring and Mitigating the Cost of Employee Turnover,* shrm.org, www.shrm.org/multimedia/webcasts/Documents/12ruyle_2.pdf.

6. High Point University, Office of the President, highpoint.edu, www.highpoint.edu/president/.

7. U.S. News Education, U.S. News & World Report, Regional Colleges Rankings, colleges.usnews.rankingsandreviews.com, http://colleges.usnews.rankingsandreviews.com/best-colleges/high-point-university-2933; http://colleges.usnews.rankingsandreviews.com/best-colleges/rankings/regional-colleges

8. High Point University, HPU's Annual Economic Impact Grows by 190 Percent to $464.5 Million (June 27, 2012), Visitor Information, highpoint.edu, http://www.highpoint.edu/blog/2012/06/hpus-annual-economic-impact-grows-by-190-percent-to-464-5-million/ /.

9. Strata Decision Technology, press release (June 13, 2012), Dan Michelson Joins Strata Decision Technology as CEO, (June 13, 2012), stratadecision.com, www.stratadecision.com/our-company/newsroom/press-releases/2012/06/13/dan-michelson-joins-strata-decision-technology-as-ceo.

10. Strata Decision Technology, press release (August 20, 2014) Strata Decision Technology Named to Inc. 5000 List of Fastest Growing Private Companies; www.stratadecision.com/our-company/newsroom/press-releases/2014/08/20/strata-decision-technology-named-to-inc.-5000-list-of-america-s-fastest-growing-private-companies.

5   Innovation: It's Not Complicated

1. Zappos!, Zappos! Core Value #1, zappos.com, http://about.zappos.com/our-unique-culture/zappos-core-values/deliver-wow-through-service.

2. Zappos!, Zappos! Core Value #1, zappos.com, http://about.zappos.com/our-unique-culture/zappos-core-values/deliver-wow-through-service.

3. DEKA Research and Development Corporation, Our Founder, dekaresearch.com, www.dekaresearch.com/founder.shtml.

4. Allscripts, press release (October 8, 2012), Allscripts Launches $1 Million Health Innovation Program, allscripts.com, http://investor.allscripts.com/phoenix.zhtml?c=112727&p=irol-newsArticle&ID=1742763&highlight=Innovation.

7   The Customer's Success Is Your Success

1. Avaya, press release (June 24, 2013), Avaya Customer Effort Impact Study Reveals thenconvenience, Avaya.com, www.avaya.com/usa/about-avaya/newsroom/news-releases/2013/pr-130624.

2. Nordstrom, press release (May 15, 2014), Nordstrom First Quarter 2014 Earnings Exceed Outlook, nordstrom.com, http://investor.nordstrom.com/phoenix.zhtml?c=93295&p=irol-newsArticle&ID=1931687&highlight=.

3. Harvard Business IdeaCast Video Podcast, The Ripple Work Effect of a Great Work Culture, learnoutloud.com, www.learnoutloud.com/podcaststream /podcast_vedio.php?url=http://feeds.harvardbusiness.org/~r/harvardbusiness /videoideacast/~5/M_R0hV4p_Yc/video.mp4&title=29898.
4. Virgin Group, About Us, virgin.com, www.virgin.com/about-us.
5. Trip Advisor Restaurant Review, The Angus Barn, Raleigh, North Carolina, tripadvisor.com, www.tripadvisor.com/Restaurant_Review-g49463-d444972 -Reviews-The_Angus_Barn-Raleigh_North_Carolina.html; Fodor's Travel, Central North Carolina, Fodor's Review, Angus Barn, fodors.com, www .fodors.com/world/north-america/usa/north-carolina/central-north-carolina /review-47237.html.

8 Paying It Forward: Giveback and Social Responsibility

1. HP Next Team Volunteer Week Is Every Week at HP (April 10, 2014), HP.com, www8.hp.com/hpnext/posts/volunteer-week-every-week-hp?jumpid =reg_r1002_usen_c-001_title_r0001#.U-ahLit17xE.
2. HP Next Team, Volunteer Week is Every Week at HP (April 10, 2014), HP.com, www8.hp.com/hpnext/posts/volunteer-week-every-week-hp#.U-Vcfit17xE.
3. John Chambers, White House and IT Industry Partnership Prepares Servicemen and Women for the Workforce, Cisco Blogs (April 29, 2013), cisco.com, http://blogs.cisco.com/news/white-house-and-it-industry-partnership-prepares -servicemen-and-women-for-the-workforce/.
4. Gallup-Healthways study, *Harvard Business Review*, Positive Intelligence (January 1, 2012), HBR.org, www.hbr.org/2012/01/positive-intelligence/ar/1.
5. *Harvard Business Review*, Positive Intelligence (January 1, 2012), HBR.org, http://hbr.org/2012/01/positive-intelligence/ar/1
6. United Healthcare/VolunteerMatch study (March 2010), Do Good Live Well: Reviewing the Benefits of Volunteering, volunteermatch.org, http://cdn.vol-unteermatch.org/www/about/UnitedHealthcare_VolunteerMatch_Do_Good _Live_Well_Study.pdf, pp. 5, 27–31.
7. Deloitte Volunteer IMPACT Research, Measuring Important Aspects of Corporate Community Engagement, deloitte.com, www.deloitte.com/view /en_US/us/About/Community-Involvement/5243f30d90750310VgnVCM 3000001c56f00aRCRD.htm; www2.deloitte.com/content/dam/Deloitte /us/Documents/us-citizenship-2011-impact-survey-employee-engagement .pdf.
8. HP, HP 2012 Global Citizenship Report (2012), HP.com, http://h20195.www2 .hp.com/V2/GetPDF.aspx/c03742928.pdf, p. 125.
9. United Healthcare/VolunteerMatch study (March 2010), Do Good Live Well: Reviewing the Benefits of Volunteering, volunteermatch.org, http://cdn. volunteermatch.org/www/about/UnitedHealthcare_VolunteerMatch_Do_Good _Live_Well_Study.pdf, pp. 5, 27–31.
10. Quicken Loans, press release, Fortune Magazine Names Quicken Loans a Top 5 Best Place to Work in America (January 16, 2014), quickenloans.com, www

.quickenloans.com/press-room/2014/fortune-magazine-names-quicken-loans -a-top-5-best-place-to-work-in-america/.

11. Deloitte Volunteer IMPACT Research, Measuring Important Aspects of Corporate Community Engagement, deloitte.com, www.deloitte.com/view /en_US/us/About/Community-Involvement/5243f30d90750310VgnVCM300 0001c56f00aRCRD.htm; www2.deloitte.com/content/dam/Deloitte/us /Documents/us-citizenship-2011-impact-survey-employee-engagement.pdf.

12. Points of Light (www.pointsoflight.org), Business for Better: The Community Partnership Movement (www.Business4Better.org), Seven Practices of Effective Employee Volunteer Programs, pointsoflight.org, www.pointsoflight.org/sites /default/files/corporate-institute/ubm_b4b_whitepaper8.pdf, p. 3.

9 Learning Is Your Edge: Invest in Your People

1. Society of Human Resources Management (www.shrm.org), 2014 Human Capital Benchmarking Report (June 2014).

2. Ross Blake, Employee Retention: What Employee Turnover Really Costs Your Company, WebProNews.com (July 24, 2006), webpronews.com, www.web pronews.com/employee-retention-what-employee-turnover-really-costs-your -company-2006-07.

3. Aberdeen Group, Analyst Insights (November 2013), The Power of Employee Recognition, aberdeen.com, http://v1.aberdeen.com/launch/report /perspective/8750-AI-employee-recognition-program.asp.

10 Leaders Who Drive Operational Excellence Net Extraordinary Results

1. Hay Group, press release (May 2, 2012), Seventh Annual Hay Group Study Identifies Best Companies for Leadership, haygroup.com, www.haygroup.com /ww/press/details.aspx?id=33718.

2. Warren Bennis, Leader to Leader (Spring 1999), leadertoleader.org, www.leader toleader.org/knowledgecenter/L2L/spring99/bennis.html.

3. Corporate Leadership Council, Driving Performance and Retention through Employee Engagement (2004), google.com, https://www.google.com/?gws_rd =ssl#newwindow=1&q=corporate+leadership+council+driving+performance+a nd+retention+AND+2010; Corporate Executive Board, The Role of Employee Engagement in the Return to Growth, Businessweek (August 13, 2010), google. com, www.google.com/?gws_rd=ssl#newwindow=1&q=corporate+leadership+ council+driving+performance+and+retention+AND+2010.

4. WRAL, Blue Cross Profits, Executive Pay Up in 2013 (February 28, 2014), WRAL.com, www.wral.com/blue-cross-profits-executive-pay-up-in-2013/1343 8661/; http://www.bcbsnc.com/content/corporate/index.htm.

5. Blue Cross Blue Shield of North Carolina, About Us, bcbsnc.org, www.bcbsnc .com/content/corporate/index.htm.

6. Cisco, Executive Bios, Carlos Dominguez, cisco.com, http://newsroom.cisco
   .com/carlos-dominguez?articleId=33353.
7. Blue Cross Blue Shield of North Carolina, press release (March 5, 2014), March
   for Enrollment: BCBSNC Reaches out to North Carolinians from the Coast
   to the Mountains, bcbsnc.com, http://mediacenter.bcbsnc.com/news?page=2;
   BCBS-NC, press release (February 28, 2014), BCBSNC Adds Customers,
   Invests to Meet Health Care Reform Requirements, bcbsnc.com, http://media
   center.bcbsnc.com/news?page=4.
8. The Ken Blanchard Companies, The High Cost of Doing Nothing: Quantifying
   the Impact of Leadership on the Bottom Line (2009), blanchard-bg.com,
   www.blanchard-bg.com/materials/Blanchard_The_High_Cost_of_Doing
   _Nothing.pdf.
9. Ibid.; Elaine D. Pulakos, Rose A. Mueller-Hanson, Ryan S. O'Leary, Michael
   M. Meyrowitz, Building a High-Performance Culture: A Fresh Look at
   Performance Management, SHRM Foundation' Effective Practice Guideline
   Series, shrm.org, www.shrm.org/about/foundation/products/Documents
   /Perf%20Mgmt%20EPG-FINAL%20for%20web.pdf.
10. Quicken Loans, press release (July 7, 2014), Five of the Best Up-and-Coming
    Areas in America, quickenloans.org, www.quickenloans.org/blog/downtown
    -revitalization/five-best-coming-areas-america;
11. Netflix, Netflix Culture: Freedom and Responsibility, slideshare.net, www
    .slideshare.net/reed2001/culture-1798664.

11 My 7 Points to Culture System of Success!

1. Kodak, About Kodak, Our Company, kodak.com, http://www.kodak.com/ek
   /US/en/Our_Company/History_of_Kodak/Milestones_-_chronology/2010
   -2014.htm.

12 Make It Happen

1. CECP/The Conference Board, Majority of Companies Increased
   Community Investments, Focused Giving Programs Since End of Global
   Recession: 261 Companies Took Part in Largest Study of Corporate Societal
   Engagement, cecp.co, (October 20, 2014), cecp.co, http://cecp.co/pdfs/
   giving_in_numbers/2014/2014_GIN_Report_PR.pdf.

Index